Y0-BSW-275

Church Planting:
This is NOT a Manual

"For which of you, intending to build a tower, does not sit down first, and count the cost, to determine if you have enough to finish it?"

Luke 14:28

BILL AGEE

Publisher *MARKIV CHURCH SOLUTIONS*
www.markivchurchsolutions.com

CHURCH PLANTING: THIS IS NOT A MANUAL. Copyright © 2018 by Bill Agee. All rights reserved. Printed in the United States of America. No part of this book may be used or reproduced in any manner whatsoever without written permission except in the case of brief quotations embodied in critcal articles and reviews. For information please contact: *MARKIV CHURCH SOLUTIONS*, 795 Heritage Avenue Clovis, California 93619.

First paperback edition published 2011.

ISBN: 978-0-9840111-0-0

† ACKNOWLEDGEMENTS

This book is the result of a team effort to bring together all the people and systems that I have had the privilege of engaging. I want to take a moment to thank the people who have spoken into my life over the years and have been willing to tell me the truth and hold me accountable. Without their input this book would not have been possible.

Before anyone else, I want to say a special thanks to my wife Pam and our children Adam and Amy. They are central to my life and to my story. They have believed in me when the choices we were making seemed strange indeed. Pam has been a tireless worker and wonderful support of the vision God gave to us many decades ago. In this writing effort as well, she has been patient and diligent as she always has been. She understands as well as anyone that church planting is truly a lifestyle and cannot be captured in a manual. As our wonderful adventure continues I am thankful to God that we can make this journey together. Together, we have faced the good with rejoicing, and faced the difficult with perseverance. I am not certain what the future holds but I am very thankful that whatever it turns out to be I will have Pam there to face it with me.

I want to thank my children for urging me to write down some aspects of this adventure. They have played a key role in this story and continue to do so as they serve the Lord with their families. They are living out the chapters of their lives and one day will be able to share their faith journeys as I have had the privilege to do here. I am very proud of them and the godly people they have become. They have been a constant joy for Pam and me as we have watched God touch their lives and as they have responded to Him.

I want to thank the people in the churches I have pastored for their trust and their confidence in me as I began to flesh out my life's calling. My first church in Mobridge, South Dakota, where I spent ten years, holds a very special place in my life. As some would say, we really "did life" together there with some of the greatest people on the planet. They prayed for me, served with me, held my arms up when I was tired and poured their lives out for the Kingdom.

I especially want to thank the people in the Central Association of Southern Baptists in Phoenix, Arizona who took a chance on me and my off the wall vision. It was there that much of the content in this book that deals with the nuts and bolts of church planting was forged. It was there that God put the pieces together for the later chapters of my ministry and helped me develop a network of people and systems that continue to hold an important place in my life and ministry. I am thankful for the time spent at the North American Mission Board where I was able to see a larger scale of what God was up to and how He was working. Relationships developed during that chapter of my life have shaped my national and global vision.

Finally, I want to thank First Baptist Church Woodstock and Pastor Johnny Hunt for believing in me and calling me to this great church where I have had the freedom and support to expand the church planting process. This is where the journey continues and I am excited for the future and what God is going to do with Pam and me on our quest to make Him known. Our faith journey continues.

✝ CONTENTS

Bill Agee

✝ FOREWORD

A book will come along from time to time that not only captures the passion and desire of your heart, but you feel it is a book that is especially written for such a time as this. That is the way I feel about *Church Planting: This is NOT a Manual* by Bill Agee. This book takes to heart Luke 14:28 where the Scripture teaches that a person desiring to build a tower should first sit down and count the cost to determine if they have what it takes to finish. This passage also applies to church planters desiring to establish a strong, healthy, reproducing church. They too must count the cost before they begin. Southern Baptists, in particular, have made a major commitment in the area of church planting. We have seen through our research throughout the nation how God has blessed and enhanced the kingdom work through the starting of new, gospel-centered churches.

When the Lord places His hand and His call upon a young man to serve as a church planter, the Lord then places him on an exciting journey. One of the things that he realizes almost immediately is the need for help and for someone to come alongside him to encourage, enlighten, and enhance the journey. God has raised up Bill Agee to be that person. Bill has served as a church-planter, Pastor of a sponsoring church, led in the development of church-planting processes, and helped find funding through foundational gifts and church partnerships for church planting. Now God has allowed him to share the truths that helped him be effective in this area to help others. This book is a picture of a true biblical disciple; one who learns at the feet of Jesus and then, in turn, teaches others that which he has received.

After sitting through three of Bill Agee's Church Planting Schools with 300 church planters I watched the excitement in their eyes and the joy begin to well up in their hearts as they began to grasp the concepts that would allow them to start in strength not in a survival mode. They designed and developed a plan that was not only something they could stick with for the long haul but it was also attainable with clearly defined mile markers along the way. I was able to clearly see the difference this teaching made in their lives and ministries.

This is a practical book. Not only is it a leadership book and a developmental book, it is a personal life story written for the express purpose of helping our new church planters get a better grasp on the work God has called them to do.

As you read this book many names and faces of young leaders you know will come to your mind. You will certainly want to get a copy of this book in their hands as quickly as you can so they too can experience the joy you found as you turned from page to page and read that which was easy to grasp in its simplicity, yet thorough in its dealing with the subject of planting gospel-centered churches.

Enjoy the journey, and make sure you take others along with you.

Pastor Johnny Hunt

✝ INTRODUCTION

The following pages are meant to revolutionize the way church planting is done in America. The title of this book *Church Planting: This is NOT a Manual* is designed to elicit curiosity from a reader who might be looking for more than a checklist of the *"how-to's"* in church planting.

In its essence this book is about faith, church planting, and how they intertwine to form a lifestyle. Church planting is more than just a one, two, or three step manual. For the church planter who as been able to establish a strong healthy church, it has been about a church planting lifestyle involving choices and decisions that ultimately lead a person back to God's call. Faith and church planting cannot and should not be separated.

I want the reader to get a glimpse into the life of my family whose exciting faith journey has highlighted church planting from virtually every angle. Pam and I, as well as our children Adam and Amy, have been engaged in establishing strong, healthy, reproducing churches in many parts of the country for over thirty years.

This book will show the way God worked in our lives through faith and how the stresses and strains of church planting played out in our lives. Being a church planter is not easy. It requires faith, perseverance, and sacrifice on everyone's part in order to be successful. Church planting is not an event, it is a lifestyle. It gets into your blood. It is evidenced most clearly when the excitement and risks of Antioch become more appealing than the safety and certainty of Jerusalem.

It is my desire to show the reader that every ministry opportunity adds another piece to the puzzle of life. In the beginning there is not much definition and more uncertainty than certainty, but as the pieces of the puzzle come together the work God is doing becomes more and more clear.

I hope to give the reader an honest and authentic look at the many aspects of church planting that often are not seen. Church planting is not the glamorous sprint that is portrayed in the world today. It is a marathon requiring focus, stamina and a certain and dynamic call from God.

There will be places in the book where you will be amazed at the provision of God and marvel at His timing. Other times you will be challenged by the difficulty of the decisions that must be made on a daily basis. There will be times of great joy and exhilaration and other times of tremendous sadness and a sense of loss as you identify with the characters in my family's story.

This book will not only provide the true and heart-warming story of a family walking a faith journey together but will also provide the practical aspects, the nuts and bolts of planting strong, healthy, reproducing churches for those engaged in that calling today.

Over the years I have, through experience and the input of many people, developed a process for church planting taken from the Scriptures known as *Count the Cost* under the umbrella of *MARKIV CHURCH SOLUTIONS*. The *Count the Cost* process will be detailed and clearly defined in high resolution detail within later chapters, so you will be able to understand how it applies to your unique situation.

Scripture teaches all of us to sit down and count the cost of what we are about to do, to determine if we can really do it. If we are not able to do what we set out to do, it can bring shame and disgrace on the work of the Lord Jesus. What the *MARKIV CHURCH SOLUTIONS Count the Cost* process allows a church planter to do is to get a glimpse into the future to see in high resolution what the road he is about to embark upon looks like and whether he has the ability to accomplish it.

It is my belief that the *Count the Cost* process will benefit any church planter regardless of his situation, circumstance, context, style, geography or culture and will provide potential sponsoring and supporting churches the ability to be the best stewards of what God has entrusted to them.

You will find that this is not a manual but it is a unique process that will give the church planter the ability to think ahead and see the potentially fatal issues that can blindside a new church and stop it in its tracks. The church planter will then be able to make wiser choices on their journey to maturity and reproduction.

✝ PART ONE:
Church Planting: Our Story

✝ CHAPTER ONE
Faith: A Life Journey

Faith is indeed a life journey. My story is about God dealing with me in the decisions of my life and how faith has played a significant role. I will attempt to tell this story with as much accuracy and honest reflection as possible. When God moves and we act in faith believing Him at His word there is no need to embellish because the acts of God are remarkable enough and do not need our help. So, with that said, let's begin the journey.

My faith journey began when I was in high school. The circumstances that led to my acknowledgement and exercise of faith were many. I was born in a small town in Oklahoma and even though we lived in the heart of the *"Bible Belt,"* our home was not a Christian home. There was a semblance of religion in our home but there was no personal relationship with God that brought about a change in behavior or lifestyle. As strange as it may seem based on the geography of where I grew up, I was almost totally ignorant of the very basics of the things of God and what it meant to have a personal relationship with Jesus. Not until I was in high school did I come face to face with the reality that I needed Jesus Christ in my life. I find it difficult to believe that in the heartland of America I went for sixteen years and was never in a situation where I could hear the Gospel and have an opportunity to respond to what I had heard. I was not a trouble maker or a mean person, in fact, I was considered a very nice and polite young man, yet I was not a follower of Jesus. On the outside I was very acceptable but on the inside I was lost.

As I grew up and entered high school I had made some friends who were nice to me and highly respected at school. They would talk to me about their church and their youth group and how much they enjoyed being a part of all the activities and Bible studies. I had no idea what a youth group was since I had only been to church a few times in my life. It sounded interesting to me and I liked being around them but I did not have a Bible and felt that I did not know enough to participate. Thankfully, they did not stop asking me to join them. I am eternally grateful for their persistence.

My Opportunity Arrives

One of my friends asked me to come to a revival at their church and then join the youth at one of their homes for something called fellowship. I had never been to a revival service and was not sure what you do to have fellowship but I wanted to be a part of this group of friends so I decided to go to the revival service with them. Little did I realize that this would be an eternity-changing decision and a pivotal moment in my life.

As the time approached for my friends to pick me up to go to the church, the more nervous I became. I was not the most outgoing person and was not sure of what to do or say. If I could have, I would have gone to my room and hidden from everyone, but that was not an option. Their car pulled up, I got in, and off we went to the church. I was terrified on the inside and tried my best not to show it.

As the service began I was trying to take in all that was happening around me. People were smiling, laughing, and seemed to be having a great time. The service started and I observed the people and my friends genuinely engaged in what was happening. They were singing and participating without any urging from anyone. They really liked being there. This was my first instance of seeing people involved in anything religious that had an effect on their life and their behavior. I was fascinated but did not know what made them feel what they felt.

The preacher began his sermon with a Bible reading and then started to explain what the verses meant and how they could be related to our lives. I had never heard anything like this and did not know what to think about it. One thing I did know was that the things he was saying spoke to me and created a hunger in me to want to know more.

As we left the service I was more curious than ever to find out more about what the preacher had said about how each person could have a personal relationship with the Son of God. On the way to the youth fellowship my friends asked me what I thought about the service. I told them that I wanted to know more about what the preacher was saying. They noticed I did not have a Bible and gave me one on the way home. They said they were going to the revival again the next night and asked me to come. I told them I would.

As the revival service started the second night I was more prepared for what was happening and eager to get to the sermon part of the service to find out more about this relationship with Jesus. Once again the preacher read a Bible verse, (I could now read along with him in my new Bible) and began to explain it.

All through the service I knew I wanted to have this relationship but I did not know how to get it. At the end of the service I asked one of my friends if he could explain to me how I could have the relationship with Jesus that the preacher had preached about for the last two nights. He happily shared with me and showed me the scripture verses and led me in a prayer of salvation.

Once I had prayed and by faith received Jesus Christ as my Savior, my life changed and has never been the same. I could not get enough of church and preaching. I loved reading my new Bible and discovering the Bible stories that everyone else had been taught as children. I had a lot of catching up to do. I could not get enough of being with my Christian friends. I had never felt loved like I now felt loved and it changed my life. A simple act of faith started me on a life journey that has been and continues to be a very exciting experience.

The remainder of my time in high school was filled with church activities and learning more and more about what the Christian life was about. My desire was to learn how to live to make a difference. At home my family continued in their lifestyle and did not want to change what they were comfortable doing. At first I sensed resistance from them and even attempts to keep me from attending some of the church activities, but over time they saw that my life had changed and that I was serious about my walk with the Lord. Even though they did not make a decision for Christ at that time in their lives they did not hinder my pursuit of God.

My Call to Ministry

As I prepared to enter college I began to sense that God was doing something in my life but I did not know what it might be. I felt there was a deeper commitment God was asking of me and that it would require a large amount of faith for me to follow Him. I had come to understand that faith involved believing and acting on something even before you could actually see it. It was just as I was entering college that I made my second great faith step and surrendered my life to serve God in a Christian ministry vocation. Not knowing exactly what God wanted for me, I began to seek Him even more and find the faith path He wanted for my life. I was both humbled that God would call me and excited about what He wanted me to do.

My decision was a shock to my family and friends. I was the quiet and shy one in my family and now God had called me to proclaim His gospel to the world. It did not make sense to the people I knew but it made sense to God. He chooses the weak things so His strength can be revealed. He wanted me to be a willing and usable vessel that He would fill and pour out for His Kingdom sake. What a responsibility and what a blessing.

God Provides a Helpmate

The next years were spent in preparation for carrying out God's call on my life. I had made up my mind that wherever He wanted me to go I would go. During my educational years God brought a young lady into my life who completely captured my heart.

Pam was from a fine Christian home and had come to know Christ at a young age. She was outgoing, sweet, and had a smile that was amazing. She was then and is today beautiful on the outside but just as beautiful on the inside. God was preparing me for the future by allowing me to serve as the associate pastor and music leader in the same church Pam attended and served by playing piano for the music ministry. The more time we spent together the more we knew that not only had God directed our paths to bring us together but God was also joining our hearts to serve Him together. After three years of dating we began to talk seriously about getting married.

Marriage is such an important faith decision in the journey of life that we did not want to miss what God was doing. After prayer, counsel from family and godly friends and seeking the face of God we knew that He was bringing us together for an amazing journey of faith.

Looking back on it now, we had no idea all God had in store for us as we served Him together. We never could have imagined that we would be privileged to see the mighty hand of God as we have seen it, or be allowed to do what we have done as His servants. We have been most blessed. I know that the call on my life would not have been complete without her there to sustain me. God knew what lay ahead for us in ministry and He gave each of us different gifts to compliment and complete the other. I am much stronger with her than I ever could be without her. She is God's greatest blessing and gift to my life and to the ministry He called us to do.

God charted the courses of our lives to bring us together for the ministry He had called us to do. Now that the union was complete and God had put us together, it was time for our journey of faith in ministry to begin.

✝ CHAPTER TWO
The Early Years of Ministry

God did not allow much time to pass before He revealed where He wanted us to serve Him. After a year of marriage we were settling into ministry in our church when we were asked to lead worship at a youth summer camp in South Dakota. While we were there we met a missionary from the Dakotas who shared with us about a small community in South Dakota where a new church should be started. A church from Arkansas had conducted a Vacation Bible School there and had purchased a small church building and a small house. The second day of the camp our pastor was called back to conduct a funeral which left the preaching responsibilities to me. God showed great favor on the messages and many young people came to Christ. The missionary approached me after the camp and asked if my wife and I would consider coming to the community of Mobridge, South Dakota to begin the new church. Without any hesitation I told him no.

Faith and Church Planting Unite

Pam and I had only been married a year and were doing well in our church and the secular job I was doing and did not even consider moving almost one thousand miles away from our parents. We left the camp, drove back home, and did not think much about the offer for a week or so. We left for our own church youth camp the following week and were looking forward to enjoying the camp, but God began to stir in each of us and brought the conversation we had with the missionary to our minds.

As the first service of the youth camp began, the theme song was entitled, *"It Takes Faith."* The words of the verses were speaking directly to us and stirring within us the desire to follow the leading of the Lord.

Counting the Cost

Pam and I talked many hours about the huge decision we were contemplating. We discussed the fact that for both of us, this would be the first time we would be a thousand miles away from anyone we knew. We talked about the drastic cut in pay we would take if we made this decision. We would be totally and completely dependent on God to literally provide the daily sustenance of food, clothing, and a way to heat the house. We would be involved in a ministry we had never done and we knew nothing about. We did not know the first step to take to plant a new church. We were going into unknown territory with only God to show us the way.

As we prayed and sought the will of God we also discussed how the hand of God was involved in this decision. We did not seek this responsibility, it came to us. God had orchestrated the circumstances at the camp to allow me the opportunity to preach and see His hand on the message as He touched many young people's lives. We were convicted and encouraged as well by the theme song at a different camp that spoke to our situation so clearly. We also knew that our hearts had been changed and the desire to pioneer the

Gospel in unknown regions was now a greater desire than to stay in the safety and comfort of our family and friends.

I thought about the Apostle Paul and his missionary journeys and how he, Barnabus, and John Mark went into hostile and unknown lands to further the Gospel. Even as John Mark departed and went back to his comfort and safety, Paul continued on. He had faced many hardships and through it all God had been faithful. We believed that God was calling us to that kind of faith and belief in Him and His provision for our lives, our ministry, and even the daily necessities.

By the end of the camp we were convinced that God wanted us to embark on a faith journey the likes of which we had never seen before.

As soon as we returned home we called the missionary and asked him if the church in South Dakota had been started yet. He told us it had not. We asked him if he still felt we should come to start the church. He said he felt that we were the people to come there and we confirmed with him that we felt God's urging to go there as well. We had never been to Mobridge, South Dakota before, but we knew that was where we were to begin our ministry.

✝ CHAPTER THREE
The Adventure Begins

In August of 1977, we loaded what belongings we had into a U-Haul truck and headed north on this grand adventure. Even though this was decades ago I can still recall as if it were yesterday, driving that U-Haul truck on the long journey to our new home and the excitement we felt. We thought about Abraham as he went out under God's leading looking for a city. We were like the pioneers heading across country we had never seen to a home waiting for us one thousand miles away.

As we got closer to Mobridge the excitement was even greater than before. We were coming to our new home and to our church building even though there were no people to help start the church. After living in a very small apartment and not having a home of our own, we were very excited to have our own house. We wondered what it would look like and where it would be located. We believed God had led us there and that He would take care of us.

As we topped the last hill and saw our community for the first time we were amazed at how beautiful it was. The community is located on the Oahe Lake which is fed by the Missouri River. There were trees, which were not very prevalent outside the community. Most of the countryside was made up of prairie and corn and sunflower fields. We drove for miles and miles and all we saw were corn fields and sunflower fields as far as you could see. The lake was about a mile wide and the community was on a peninsula. Mobridge was a community of 3,000 people and was the largest community for 100 miles in any direction. We were thrilled to get to our house.

Things Are Not Always What They Seem

We looked around for the location of our house and the church building where we would start the church. We had an address but that did not help us very much since we did not know how the community was laid out and did not have a city map. As we drove around and saw our new community for the first time it was very well maintained and the houses and the yards were beautiful. We saw some very nice areas of town that were well taken care of and showed pride of ownership but ultimately found the church building and our tiny house in a section of town that was far from what we thought it would be. The properties had been neglected and were in need of repair. What we thought would be waiting for us was not there. Our visions of what our home and our neighborhood would be were not what we found. It would take significant work just to make the spaces usable.

With reality not matching up with expectations we were wondering about our decision to go so far from familiar surroundings and friends to a place we had never seen. Those feelings were short-lived and we launched into this new faith adventure with all we had. After finishing the much needed repairs, painting, and sprucing up of the house, our attentions were turned to the church building. We realized the church was an old Wesleyan Church and did not have a baptistry. Later we found that it also did not have any insulation in the walls or the ceiling. That made for some cold services that first winter until we were able to insulate it properly. Each day it became more apparent that our expectations were very different than the reality in which we were living.

There was also a stark contrast in my personal life as I was trying to start a church with the message of life and hope, while my other job working with the funeral director always involved tragedy, sadness, and death.

J.D. Kesling was the funeral director whose business was across the street from the house where we lived and the church building where we held our worship services. J. D. was in his eighties at the time and was, on the outside, crusty and stern but inside he had a heart of gold. He was one of the first people we met when we came to town and soon we discovered his love for the Native American people living just across the river. Many of the funerals were Native Americans whose families had little if anything to pay for the funeral. That did not stop J.D. He would load the body in the small plane he flew, land on the highway near where the funeral would be held, place the body for viewing, complete the burial, taxi back to the highway and fly home. Hardly ever did he get paid for the services he offered.

I certainly had not anticipated working in a funeral home to support my family, but that is what happened. God used that experience in many ways.

The church in Arkansas that had originally held the Vacation Bible School and saw the need for a new church had committed $300 per month to a salary (which by the way was the salary). This really looked like it was going to be a faith venture. And it was.

With only $300 per month we were not going to be able to purchase much at the stores for our needs. As it turned out we ate what we could grow, catch, and shoot. Fish, deer, and pheasant became staples in our diet and we grew vegetables in our garden to can and freeze. We were learning more each day that we must be committed to doing whatever it took to make a difference for the Kingdom.

God provided other needs in some significant and unusual ways. He allowed us in the very early stages of our faith journey to see Him in action. Our first real financial decision came soon after we arrived. We were now self-employed and as a result had to provide our own health insurance. When that first bill arrived showing the cost of the first three months totaling $234.90, we were shocked and concerned since our entire salary was $300 per month. We prayed together and told the Lord we knew He had called us there and was able to do more than we could ask or think. We were fine with Him providing the amount needed but we were also fine with simply trusting Him to keep us healthy. In any event we had five days to determine what we would do. Over the next five days we received in the mail several checks from people we had never met and would not hear from again that totaled $235.00. At that time stamps were ten cents so we knew what God was saying to us. We thankfully paid the bill and never had another issue with health insurance. God always provided.

That story may seem a little strange but it is not any stranger than when Abraham took Isaac up on the mountain and at the time he was about to slay his son he looked and saw a ram caught in a thicket. He used the ram for the sacrifice instead of his son. The interesting thing to me about that story is that the ram was ascending the mountain from one side at the same time Abraham and Isaac were ascending it from the other side. God's timing is amazing. In our case the people who sent the money had to have sensed God's direction to do this for a total stranger at a certain time before the need was even known, in order for it to get to us on time. God's faithfulness is unbounded. There were many instances where God had to show up for us to make it and He always did.

We also learned that God is faithful even when circumstances are different than what we thought they would be. It was a good lesson that has been needed many times in our lives and ministry. Our ways are not always God's ways.

Upon our arrival in town we placed an ad in the local weekly newspaper announcing Sunday morning services at the new Mobridge Southern Baptist Church. We did not know what to expect as Sunday rolled around. Would anyone show up? Would they be hostile or glad we were there? There were a few people from our home church that had traveled with us to help us move so we knew there would be some people in attendance.

When Sunday arrived the crowd consisted of our family and friends and five other people from the community. One was a police officer who was the son of a Southern Baptist missionary and the other was a young family of four who were looking to find a church where they would hear the Bible preached and their children would have a place to grow up in the Lord. These five people became the core of our church for several months. Each Sunday there would be a new four or five people in attendance but often not the same four or five.

The Breakthrough

In January of 1978 on a very cold and snowy Sunday morning, we went over to the church to prepare for the service. In January the temperatures seldom move above 0° for highs. The snow was many inches deep since the snow did not melt from the time it fell in early November until sometime in April and the streets were coated with an ice sheet several inches thick. I was not sure anyone would try to get out on a day like that.

I had been out all night retrieving a body for the funeral director. After digging out of the snow drifts on several occasions I finally arrived at home with just enough time to take a shower and make my way over to the church building for the morning service.

As the time for services approached, cars began to drive up and park on the street around the church. By the time church started there were 42 people in the building. We had not seen a crowd like that in the five months the church had been in existence. All of the 42 were made up of young families with children. You can imagine our excitement. Pam and I had visited people in many homes in our neighborhood and around the town for months and had knocked on many doors. In most cases when someone answered the knock at the door, we were told *"We are Catholic or Lutheran and so is the whole block so there is no need to bother asking any of them."* Pam and I would politely thank them and move on to the next house only to be told the same thing.

Now it seemed God was showing His favor for our faithfulness to continue to share His story. All the next week we followed up on these young families. We spent time in their homes and heard their stories and fell in love with each of them. With great anticipation we prepared for the next Sunday. Every week, without fail, we had prepared and I had put together a message as if the entire community was coming and on that day it seemed they did. If we were not ready for God to send a harvest the outcome might have been different. The next Sunday 54 people attended and three weeks later 75. This was the maximum capacity of the church building.

An Amazing Discovery

For the next several weeks we followed up with visits, finding out why the people had come and asking them if they had a personal relationship with Jesus Christ. They said over and over that it was because of the Bible preaching they had heard their grandparents talk about but had not experienced themselves.

When I heard them tell me their reason for coming it made perfect sense to me because of some of the visits I had made in the community. I would often go downtown to the main street where the elderly men would be sitting and visiting together. I would introduce myself and ask them about their lives and their families. Many of them had a personal relationship with Jesus Christ. I asked them how they came to hear about Jesus. They talked about the brush arbor evangelistic meetings at the turn of the century. They would gather each evening and hear the sermons. Many of them gave their lives to Jesus as young men but there was not a church in town that was preaching about the personal relationship with Jesus. There was not an opportunity for them to begin the discipleship process. Their children had grown up in the churches in the community and were religious but without Christ. The young families were not in any church but had heard their grandfather or grandmother talk about their experience with Jesus and they had not seen it or heard it preached. I did not realize it at the time but I was doing what a church planter must do to understand his context and culture and speak into that situation with the Gospel.

When we came to town preaching the message of Jesus and His sacrifice on the cross for the sins of mankind and that He is the only way of salvation, the word spread quickly that the message grandfather had talked about was now being preached in their community. As a result we had many who came and gave their lives to Christ and the church was off and running. Our faith was very quickly becoming sight. The prayers of many in the community were being answered. Someone had come to bring them Good News that could and would save their soul.

Baby Steps for the New Church

After only five months we had a church full of young families like ourselves who were eager and hungry for the Word of God. Many of them had made a profession of their faith in Jesus Christ and needed to follow Him in baptism. There was only one problem: our building had no baptistry and it was -20° outside. We set a baptism service for May at the river and let the community know it was happening. When May came, there were twenty-six people to be baptized.

On the day of the baptism we gathered at the river in the balmy 40° weather with the water temperature at 42°. To our amazement more than one hundred people from the community came to view the baptism. I took the opportunity to share with all those in attendance just what baptism meant and what those being baptized had done. The outdoor baptisms became a regular event for the new church and each time people from the community would attend they would hear the Gospel and see it in picture form. This was a great picture of what happened at Jesus' baptism. People came and saw His baptism and heard God proclaim that this was His Son in whom He was well pleased. In our community people had come and for many had heard the Word of God in truth and clarity for the first time in their lives.

As the new church was beginning to take its first baby steps I found that in my own heart and life God was doing a work. I knew nothing of planting churches or pastoring. I was literally learning on the job. I had a fairly solid base of Biblical knowledge although I had never been to seminary. My beliefs were being tested and, through the fire, refined. Each person I interacted with, each opportunity to share the Gospel and every story I heard from people in my community were all shaping me for the ministry God had called me to fulfill.

I felt the tremendous responsibility and burden for the people God had entrusted to me. Pam and I sought the face of God and asked Him to give us wisdom and understanding so we could be what we needed to be to the new believers and to the community as a whole. I quickly found myself in situations where I needed to make decisions that would affect the future of the church and I did not have the answers. I was driven to God's Word where I knew the answer had to be for the situation. This proved to be my *"backside of the desert degree."* I was studying God's Word and immediately living it out in my life as I ministered to those God brought my way.

In each situation I found God's direction and the courage to stand on what He said in His Word. The answer was not always received well by those who were inquiring but they respected the fact that I had sought God and His Word for the answer and was not relying solely on my own opinion.

Often the issue was one of doctrine since the people did not have a solid background of knowledge about the Bible. Each time I was able to speak into their lives the truth of God's teaching and over time it had an effect on many of them. In each situation I found myself growing in my faith and my trust in God. I believed that God would give clear direction in every circumstance if I would diligently seek His face and live out what He was teaching me. It seemed that as I was able to grow and exercise my faith in God the church was able to grow with me.

During this very intense time in the ministry my greatest place of refreshment and comfort was my wife. She was always a great source of my strength and courage. I knew I could face the sometimes unbelievably difficult situations knowing that I always had her support and her love. She willingly sacrificed a great deal to provide for me what I needed, to be able to live out God's call. There were many times she was neglected and her needs were put aside. Most of those times I was so caught up in what I was trying to deal with that I did not even realize what I had done. In my haste to be everything to everyone I lost sight for a while of what was really important. For that I sought her forgiveness and in her graceful way she forgave me and we were brought closer as a result. Thankfully I learned this lesson well and in later ministry positions attempted to keep a better balance between family and ministry.

A faith journey is comprised of many different points of faith. One great example is found in the life of David. David knew by faith he could slay the Philistine because he had already seen God at work when he was able to slay the lion and the bear. As I was able to see God work in situation after situation I became more confident in my belief that He would work in the next situation I would face. My faith was growing with every circumstance. Each faith moment built on the previous one and over time created a reservoir of experiences where God showed up in a mighty way and showed His power. When His power is shown in our weakness He is then able to receive all the glory and honor that He so rightly deserves. When you see God's power and provision time after time, your faith is stronger and more confident with every challenge.

✝ CHAPTER FOUR
The Baby Church Grows Up

As I grew in courage, strength and wisdom, the church God had entrusted to me began to grow in the same way. People who just a few months prior had no personal knowledge of a personal God were beginning to believe Him for things they never would have thought about earlier.

One of the greatest needs the new church had was more worship space. More people were coming than the facility could hold. Once again we found ourselves in a faith moment when we must trust that God will do what needs to be done to further the work of the Kingdom.

Soon after the church body entered into intentional prayer for the space needs of the church, one of the church members felt the leadership of God to donate two acres of land on the north side of town to the church. This was prime property and something that the church itself had no ability to obtain apart from the moving of God's Holy Spirit in people's lives. It was similar to the story in Acts where the people were praying for Peter while he was in jail. Suddenly a knock comes at the door and when the door is opened there stands Peter but no one really believes it is him. They did not expect God to answer their prayers that quickly and that dramatically. Perhaps we were the same way. We asked God specifically and when He specifically answered we were surprised. But, we would not be surprised the next time God intervened. The church was beginning to believe in a God that worked on their behalf and in their lives.

The new church now had a piece of property where a permanent home could be built. The only problem was that we did not know how to go about it and did not have the resources to do it. Once again the new church found itself in a faith moment. I found myself not only feeling inadequate but actually being inadequate. That was where I needed to be so that I would trust completely in God and not in my abilities. The baby church needed a new building but how could it possibly happen? All we knew to do was take our need to the Lord and by faith believe that He would do what would bring honor to the Father. We did not believe He gave us a piece of property without a plan to supply what we needed to complete the work.

In January of 1979 a group of church members who had been selected to form a building committee to study what would need to be done to provide space for the church to grow, was meeting in our home when a knock came at the door. We were not expecting anyone and certainly did not think many people would be out socializing in the frigid temperatures.

I opened the door and a gentleman and his wife were standing outside. He introduced himself in such a drawl that I knew he was not from the north but had to be from the very deep south. He introduced himself and said he was from Sweetwater, Tennessee. It took many syllables to say what he said. He said he was a builder and wondered if our church had any building plans in the future.

We invited him into our home and told him this was truly something of God since we had met to discuss exactly what he was there to find out. Each person eagerly shared their hopes and dreams for a new facility and before the evening was over a rough idea of what would ultimately become the new church building was formed. Cecil, the gentleman from the south, told us that he would go to his hotel and draw some plans and would like to meet again the next evening.

What a shock to come together the next evening and have laid before us the drawings and plans for the new building. There is no way to describe the excitement in everyone's voices as they talked about what the new church could mean to us. Situations would occur where there was no way to move ahead apart from an intervention from God. The people of the church would pray and God would somehow answer their prayers. I was seeing a mighty faith army being created every day.

Cecil finally spoke and told us about what the new church would cost and that if we had the supplies on site by July he would bring a crew back and build our new church for us.

We had exactly zero dollars but again we were faced with a faith moment where we needed to step out where there was nowhere to step and believe what we could not see. I told Cecil that we would have the materials on site and that he should plan to come back in the summer. With that said, he left to go back to Tennessee.

What Now?

It did not take long to realize we had moved into a whole new realm of faith that we had not yet experienced. We knew God could handle certain things but we had never seen Him move in something this large.

Knowing the amount of money needed for the building I went to the local banks and told them our story and asked for a loan. The banks did not laugh at me but I believe they wanted to. They told me they could not do the loan since two other churches had closed their doors in recent years. I pleaded with them and told them God was at work and that He would provide, but they would have none of it.

Time was moving on and I needed to secure the funding for the new building before Cecil came back. I approached the Home Mission Board but was told there was no money available to loan for new churches in what were called pioneer areas.

Still time was moving on. I went back to the bank and told them that we needed to make this work and what would it take for them to loan us the money. They told us we needed other strong churches to sign the note and agree to pay the payment if our church was not able to do so. I learned that new churches do not qualify since they do not have a five year track record and usually little collateral. I approached the churches I knew and thankfully two of them agreed and the bank said they would give us the loan but it would take several months to close. I did not have several months. The trusses and other supplies Cecil told us needed to be on the site took time to build and deliver. I had to order the materials on faith and believe that they would be paid for when they were ready.

A Defining Faith Moment

I was faced with the greatest faith moment of my young ministry at this point. I ordered all the materials for our church and signed a personal note to be paid in sixty days. Needless to say this was a major point of prayer for me, my wife, and my young congregation over the next sixty days.

Pam and I did what we always did and took our needs to the Lord. We talked about the debt we would have and no money to pay for it should the loan not be approved. We worried about the testimony of the church and for my credibility as a pastor. Many thoughts raced through our minds but when it came right down to it, the issue was a faith issue. Did we truly believe God was leading us in this direction? We believed He was and we determined we were going to trust Him again with literally everything.

As things happen there were delays in the paperwork for the loan and the creditors were in position to come and get me when we received the word from the bank that the loan was funded. The news came two hours before Cecil's crew arrived to build the church. God proved to be faithful and on time as He always is, even though I was wondering if He was going to show up. Once again my faith was expanded and strengthened. As I shared the information about the loan, the delays and the fact that God came through just in time, Cecil and his crew rejoiced with us over the provision and faithfulness of God.

As the sun rose on Monday morning the work started on the new church. The basement had been dug and the footings poured before the crew arrived. By Wednesday night the crew had taken the new church from a hole in the ground to a roof over our head and we paused long enough on Wednesday night to have a prayer meeting in our new space.

Cecil's crew stayed until Saturday when another crew arrived to help finish out the interior. The church was the talk of the town. No church had built anything in decades and everyone drove to the north side of town on the main street to see the spectacle. After the crews left we spent the next several months completing the interior and doing some landscaping outside. By winter of that year we were meeting in our new church building which was a miracle of God in every sense of the word.

The Church Earns Credibility

Not only were we beginning to believe God more, but people in the community began to believe in us more. Early in our ministry the people were skeptical of us because they were not sure who Southern

Baptists were and what they thought they knew was not accurate. Now the people in town were more accepting of us because they knew we were there to stay and they had seen that this church was indeed different than what they had experienced before.

God continued to draw people to the church and bring them into the Family of God. In fact there were several people driving from other communities many miles away to attend our church because the Gospel was not available to them in their communities. The church began to pray about what we could do to provide a church for those in the other communities who were driving so far. It was determined that we would start a new church in that town and the people attending our church from there would be the nucleus to start it. This was another moment of faith. People who were leaders and supporters of our church would be leaving and starting a new church. What would that mean for our church? Again we had to come to a place where God would need to come through for us to make it, yet we all knew this was the right thing to do.

We were reminded of Peter when he stepped out of the boat to go to Jesus. Had God not intervened he would have sunk into the sea and drowned. It was Peter's faith and belief in God and His provision that allowed him to walk on the water and go to Jesus. We were stepping out of the boat perhaps a little more tentatively than Peter but we were nonetheless stepping out.

The Church Has a Baby

The new church was started in a town 30 miles west of our church. It was also across a time zone. In the early days I would finish preaching at the home church at noon, drive 30 minutes, and start at 11:30a.m. That was nice but the trip home was a long one because I lost the hour on the way back. In this new church effort God once again showed that He would always provide what was needed. Each church was blessed and our faith was stretched.

This was not the only baby the church would have, in fact, there were several more. As easy as the first one was, the second one was just as difficult. This new church was located 20 miles east of the mother church in a small community. There was nowhere to meet for services. Again the church was faced with a faith moment. What would we do? Must the church cease attempting to start any more new churches since a place to meet in the smaller communities would always be a serious issue? After much prayer it was determined the church would again step out on faith and purchase a mobile home to ensure there was a place to meet. The men of the church renovated the mobile home providing for a kitchen in the front, seating for fifty, a bathroom, and a study for the pastor in the back. Once the new church grew large enough it was able to secure a facility in that community and the mobile chapel was moved to the next community where a new church was needed. The church had stepped out and God met it there.

Pam and I are Blessed With a Baby

Pam and I had been in South Dakota for several years and had been praying about starting a family. When the news came that Pam was pregnant we were so excited. We prayed for the new baby, its health, its life, its future spouse, and anything else we could think of at the time.

All throughout the pregnancy we prayed and believed God for a healthy baby. This was before parents could know the sex of their new baby but we did not care if it was a boy or a girl.

Just before the time the baby was to be born we headed to the new church building for Sunday services to be followed by a baptism service at the lake. Just as the service started, Pam indicated she was starting to have contractions but they were light and far apart, so she went on to play the piano for the service. After the service we boarded the bus to drive to the lake for a lengthy baptismal service. The contractions were closer and more intense by the time we got home. After a bit of rest it was time for the evening service, so off we go. When we got home from church that night Pam started doing laundry, cleaning house, packing, taking a shower, and calmly going through this entire process, doing everything she should not be doing in order to have everything done and be ready to go to the hospital. I kept telling her to stop working, we need to go now, *"Is it time yet? Let's go to the hospital now!"* I was feeling anything but normal.

About midnight the contractions were fairly close and pretty intense so we got in the car to go to the hospital. Thankfully both of our children were born in the summer. A winter baby in a South Dakota snow storm could mean you deliver it yourself if you cannot get to the hospital. I did not want that to happen. Believe me, neither of us wanted that to happen.

We made it to the hospital and after several hours of intense labor the most wonderful thing happened, Adam was born into our family. He was strong and healthy and we were so thankful. God had once again shown up in a remarkable way. At that moment our lives changed forever.

Three years later God blessed us with our second child. The same praying went on but this time we were a little more specific. We were asking God for a little girl. Again God showed His great favor and Amy was born into our family. We felt complete and so blessed.

We were so excited and over the years continue to thank God for the precious children He gave us. They have grown up and have families of their own and their love for God is strong and for that we praise and thank the Lord. We have been and still are so proud of each of our children and what God has done and is doing in their lives.

The Church Ministers in the Community

Having just given birth to a new church in a different town, the members of the home church were excited but focused on the people God kept bringing into the church and those who still needed to be reached. There was no difficulty with people coming, but the church also wanted to take the Gospel message outside the walls and touch people who had not yet come to the church or possibly may never come to a church building. How could it be done effectively in our context?

Several possibilities were discussed and one of them turned out to be extremely effective. It was decided that people from our church would teach the courses needed for people to receive their GED. I taught Math and History and others in our church taught the other subjects. When a student could pass one particular section of the test at our church we would then have them take the test for the school administration. Once the tests were passed, a time was set for the Commencement services. There were people in the classes who were bartenders, waiters and waitresses, and people who had not been to school in over forty years.

When the commencement day came the church rented caps and gowns for the students, all of whom had never walked across the stage to receive a diploma. They had been told to invite their family and friends all of whom had never trusted Jesus Christ as their Savior. When the pomp and circumstance began there was not a dry eye in the house as they filed in and took their places.

When it came time for the commencement address I felt led of God to speak on an academic theme but still clearly share the Gospel. I shared a simple message on four things God does not know. The first point was God does not know a person He does not love. The second point was God does not know a sin He does not hate. The third point was God does not know a better plan of salvation and the fourth point was God does not know a better time than right now to accept His salvation. Word of this ministry spread like wildfire throughout the community and people we did not know were stopping us on the street and at the grocery store to tell us what the GED ministry had meant to them and their family. Our phones started to ring off the hook with people trying to find out when the next session of classes would begin. They did not want to miss their opportunity. More and more our church was impacting all areas of our community. We had found an avenue that allowed us to share the Gospel and meet a clearly unmet need in the community.

Another key outreach in our community involved the 4th of July. Our town had a city square that was the focal point for a grand 4th of July parade. The parade was fun and it was great to see the floats and hear the music but it seemed incomplete. Our church decided to host a 4th of July *God and Country* concert in the city square immediately following the parade. At first we were met with resistance from the city council fearing that we would create some issue for them with the other churches but when no issue arose they granted us the permit to host the concert. We did not want the concert to be an end in itself so we also hosted a barbecue immediately following the concert for all who wanted to stay. Beginning the next evening the people who came to perform at the concert led our church and anyone in the community that wanted to attend in a series of evangelistic meetings.

The concert was amazing, the barbecue was fantastic and the evangelistic meetings were always well attended since the people had already heard the music and wanted to hear more. The day came when the city asked us to make the concert an annual event and they would even help with some of the cost for the barbecue. The church took advantage of every opportunity to get the Gospel message out.

The church was known by its desire to minister to the community with the love of Jesus in a tangible way. Scripture states that they will know we are Christians by our love. Love was being shown in a tangible and effective way through the ministries of the church to every person we met regardless of their standing in the eyes of others.

By now the church was known as the church that cared about people. Our crowds on Sunday morning continued to increase until there was no more room. We had arrived at another faith moment. The church needed to move to two Sunday Schools to accommodate all the people. What would that do to our fellowship? Would we have enough teachers? All were serious questions for which I had no answer. After seeking God it was decided to move to two Sunday Schools. God provided the teachers and the church took another growth spurt. Everyone was excited but knew that the current facility could not handle the number of people wanting to be involved in a Bible study on Sunday morning. Very quickly, space had once again become an issue.

Knowing that a new educational space needed to be provided I made the rounds again to find a loan to make it happen. This time it was not going to be easy since the economic climate was not conducive to churches getting loans. Interest rates were extremely high and money was scarce. The churches that signed with us on the first loan needed to be released to grow their own ministries. It appeared that everything was lining up in opposition to us moving forward with the new facility. It simply did not look like we were going to be able to expand our facilities. I had exhausted all the possibilities I knew of. Now we waited and we prayed. God had answered our prayers so many times but this seemed very difficult.

God Gives the Church a Miracle

Knowing this was a critical stage of our church's journey, the facilities became a focused point of prayer.

Then, one day, out of the blue, I received a phone call from a person I had never met who had heard about our situation and wanted to learn more. Jerry was a banker by trade and worked for a Christian entrepreneur with a heart for helping evangelistic churches provide the space they need to reach and disciple people for Christ. I told Jerry our story and he flew to our city to meet with our church. He stated that anyone can build a building. What they were interested in was establishing evangelism stations. Our church had been a leader in baptisms and had a strong evangelistic ministry in place to continue to reach people.

Jerry met with his Board and determined to loan us the money to pay off our initial loan and give the second loan all at 0% interest. That's right 0% interest! The church would make a payment equal to what an amortized loan for 20 years would be but every dollar went to principal. Our church would be paid for in five years not twenty years, and even better, the money we paid every month went to help another church like ours have their vision become a reality. We were getting our new building paid off in five years and helping a new church in the process. Wow, were we excited!

The only issue in the way was getting a construction loan from a local bank to front the funds until the building was constructed. Once the building was in place the loan with Jerry's company would be activated.

Jerry being from a banker's background knew what we would face at the bank. They said our church did not have the collateral to get the loan. Jerry gave them a number to call which was the number for his entrepreneurial boss. When they came back they simply said when do you need the money? God was so faithful in everything the church sought to do as we sought to give Him the glory for what was done.

We built the second building using the skilled people God had brought to our church since the first building was built. There were plumbers, electricians, finishers, boom truck operators and encouragers to help us when the work was hard and long. The ladies of the church kept us in food like fried chicken, strudel, brownies and all the essential food groups when you are working hard.

The building was completed and many years later if you talk to those who were there at that time, they will tell you that the spirit in the church was as sweet during that hard work as any time in the life of the church. The fellowship was in the work and the people had a mind to work. What a blessing it was to be their pastor.

The Church Reaches Out

The people were so creative and willing to do anything needed to reach people and bring glory to the Lord Jesus. They utilized what they had when resources were limited. For example, one great outreach was just before deer hunting season. Deer hunting in South Dakota is not just a sport but rather a necessity if there is going to be food on the table. Every child from twelve years old and older wants to carry their own gun and bag their own deer. Knowing this is so important, the church sent an invitation to a Gun Safety and Gun Sighting Clinic to every family that had a twelve year old child or older. The Game, Fish, and Parks personnel were ecstatic about having the opportunity to provide gun safety instructions to those beginning their first hunting season.

The people of the church provided registration and refreshments and while people were waiting for their turn, talked to them and told them the church was providing this for them free of charge. In many cases the opportunity was there and seized upon to share the Gospel.

On another occasion the high school wrestling team, which included several wrestlers from the church, won the state championship. The church invited all the wrestlers, coaches, school staff, and their families to a banquet honoring the wrestlers. People were so grateful and did not realize that churches did this sort of thing. Again the love of Christ was being demonstrated in a very tangible and effective way and new relationships were being established. And it did not cost a fortune to have the banquet.

Toward the end of our time there as pastor God led us into a ministry that would require a great deal of faith and a great deal of work which was nothing new to this congregation. Times in our nation were hard and in our community bordering on the Sioux Indian Reservation, times were especially difficult.

There were ongoing tensions between the white man and the Indians living in the area. Years earlier there had been visible expressions of the tension that existed at Wounded Knee and other locations. The Indian was skeptical and untrusting of the white man and for good reason. The white man in many instances had taken advantage of the Indian people and hurt them in the process. The church sought to bridge the barriers and establish an ongoing and godly relationship with the Indian people. The church conducted many ministries targeted to the needs of the Indian people. Food distribution was a critical issue for them.

Often there would be twenty people living in a two bedroom house and food was scarce. The city and the government helped as many as they could, but certain guidelines and restrictions would not allow them to help all that needed help. Our church was asked if we could help with feeding some of the people that fell through the cracks in the system. Without hesitation our people took on this monumental task. When word came to our church of a house full of people needing meals, the people in the church prepared the number of meals needed and delivered them to the home. What a ministry and what an opportunity to share the Gospel. The church continued to add to its reputation as a church that cared for people.

Over the next few years the church had the opportunity to establish several other churches in communities around the home church within a sixty mile circle. The church was reaching people, discipling people, and deploying people. Seeing the DNA of the home church being spread throughout the region was an exciting thing to behold and very humbling to know that God had entrusted the leadership of that church to me. For that trust I will be forever grateful.

✝ CHAPTER FIVE
God Calls to a New Assignment

After almost ten years as pastor of the church in South Dakota where planting churches had been a way of life, there came a time when I felt God moving and stirring in my heart with a different place He wanted me to serve. He had worked in my life in such a wonderful way and had grown my faith beyond anything that I could have imagined. Now, for some reason known only to Him it was time to say farewell to the only church I had ever pastored.

I had watched them come to a saving knowledge of Jesus Christ. I had seen them grow and commit their gifts and talents to His Kingdom work, and I had seen them sacrifice and give of themselves so that others would be able to hear the Gospel. I had seen their children and mine born and grow up. I had seen them learn how to minister with the Gospel in a dynamic way. How do you walk away from that? Humanly I do not think you can but when you sense God's call to begin a new faith journey you must say yes and move on.

This was a very difficult time for us. This ministry was all we had known and through it we experienced tremendous challenges and blessings. Even though we believed God would use us in a different place, it was hard to let go of such a wonderful part of our lives.

This place represented so many firsts in our lives and ministry. For us, it was the first place we were really on our own and at a point we had to trust God with our very lives. This was my first church, my first baptism, my first building project, my first church to plant. It was where my children were born. This was a church where in almost ten years I did not have a single funeral to conduct. But the time came when we had to say good-bye.

So, we closed that chapter of our lives and became excited about what God had next for us. We anticipated how our faith would be expanded. Little did I know then how much of what I had learned about the faithfulness of God I was going to need in my new assignment. I can honestly say that everything God did in my life in the previous ten years would need to be drawn upon to deal with what was about to begin.

A Whole Different Ball Game

In South Dakota there were no people in the church when we arrived, so we had never dealt with a pastor search team. I had no idea what to expect or what was expected of me. It turned out to be a very interesting dance. I was thirty three years old and had no experience in the customs or practices of a *"Bible Belt"* church. The search committees asked many questions and Pam and I told them our convictions of what we believed God was doing in our lives. It was a time for us to recommit to what our core beliefs were and not compromise anything just to please someone on the search team. They were a bit surprised by the questions I asked them. I later discovered that I was the sixty-seventh candidate they had considered to become their pastor. There was never agreement on the other sixty-six people. Nevertheless, after several conversations and visits with the church, the call was issued for me to become the pastor. When the vote was taken it was 99% approval with only two no votes. Over the years I realized these two people voted no on everything as a matter of principle.

My new assignment from God was in Oklahoma and completely different from what I had known for the last ten years. The community was home to the University of Oklahoma. Having grown up in Oklahoma this was very exciting for me. On my first Sunday as I headed into the building I recognized one of the greeters at the door. I had played high school football against him many years before. He was much larger than me and as I recall, he knocked me down several times in our game. I am sure he did not remember me but I remembered him. I walked over to him and told him that he used to knock me down but now that I was his pastor he needed to watch out for me. We reminisced for a while and became very good friends.

This was a church that was over thirty years old and had history and heritage of which I was not a part. Where they had been for the last several years was not my vision for the church and not theirs either. It was now my responsibility to share my vision, expand it and move it forward.

It was also a church that had come to a place where growth had virtually ceased. They had a beautiful auditorium, nice buildings, wonderful facilities and plenty of activities. Many of the people were content with attending worship but for the most part were not actively engaged in ministry. This was something I had not known before. For the past ten years there was always a drive to reach out and God always placed challenges before us and worked in our lives to help us to overcome them by faith. Here was a situation where I was not sure faith had been given much thought in quite some time. I knew immediately that God was going to have to show up in a strong way for me to be able to lead this congregation on a faith journey. I knew then that I was in the right place at the right time in the center of God's will.

There was a tension going on inside my spirit that was a constant battleground. God had moved in such a mighty way in South Dakota and provided when it looked like there was no way. He had allowed us to grow and multiply the church. Would that be possible here? I had to fight the urge to compare the two places. I had to take this attitude to God and ask Him to give a free spirit and a clear vision. This was not South Dakota and never would be what I had known before, nor should it be. After all, South Dakota was not what I expected it to be when I first arrived.

After wrestling with this for some time I came to a place of peace and knew that God had me there for a specific purpose. Even though He would work in different ways in my life and ministry, the ways He chose to work in this situation were just as exciting as what I had experienced in my first ministry assignment. He had placed me in a situation where I once again had to completely trust Him and allow Him to develop my ministry.

Getting the Lay of the Land

As I was getting settled into this new church, I found the church members to be wonderful people who were willing to do anything they could to help you. I also found that they had a heart for God and wanted to see His Word preached and lives changed. I was very encouraged and thankful to be there and was looking forward to what God wanted to do.

It did not take long to see that amidst the many great things God was doing in the church there were some issues that needed attention if the church was going to move forward and make an impact on this very strategic city. I remembered the story of Paul and his desire to win Rome. He felt if he could win Rome he could win the world. This church was one of those kinds of churches in that kind of city.

One of the first issues the church faced was an economic one. Knowing that economic issues can have serious long term consequences, this situation that had been left unchecked for quite some time, needed to be addressed. There was no money available for carrying out the ministries and some vital things were in jeopardy.

An examination of the records found several key issues that had contributed to the church experiencing financial shortages. For some, there was definite and concrete information and obvious conclusions could be drawn. For others, there was nothing that could be pinned down but in your heart you sensed something was amiss. As the pastor I relied on God's Spirit and my instincts to move forward.

Most of the problem was procedural and when new procedures were implemented the financial situation began to turn around. For example: the church did not have any money counting procedures and left itself open to being taken advantage of if someone chose to do so. Also, there was a shortage of accurate and understandable accounting processes. Within the church there were many capable people who were more than willing to step forward and help address this very important issue. Through their diligence and hard work, new procedures and policies were drawn up and implemented that allowed the church to operate openly and with full disclosure. Openness led to confidence and the church members began to have greater confidence in how their resources were being tracked and utilized.

In order to get a handle on the income versus outgo problem, hard choices had to be made. With priorities being established as to what received support and what did not, some people's feelings were hurt. When the ministry close to their heart was not funded they took it personally and harbored ill feelings for the ministries that had support.

Part of the problem was spiritual and when God began to work in the hearts of the people as it related to stewardship, the church took giant steps forward. For the people in the church responsible for the finances this was a blessing for them to see progress. They had remained faithful and prayerful and stood in the gap for many years. They saw their prayers answered and their faithfulness honored.

As I stated earlier, I knew God was going to have to show up in a strong way for the church to make the impact it needed to make. While we were praying for God to give us wisdom and insight into our financial situation He did something that caused everyone to take notice.

At a crucial time when the church was attempting to begin to reach out to the community and bringing the facilities into a better condition utilizing as little finances as possible God provided a significant amount of money from a forgotten source.

A church member had passed away several years before and the estate had been in litigation. The church had basically forgotten about it even though they were named as a beneficiary. Just when the church needed finances to move forward and just as the church had acted biblically to clear up the financial issues it faced, the estate was settled. Not only did the church receive the trust funds that would provide ongoing financial resources for ministry it received a lump sum of the accrued interest for the previous several years. The church had decided to move out on faith and God provided abundantly more than we could ever ask or think. The church now had the resources to bring the facilities up to speed and initiate some serious outreach into the community. The faith journey had begun and the excitement level was extremely high.

There were other extremely difficult issues the church dealt with early in the journey. Suffice it to say, had those serious issues not been addressed and those difficult decisions not been made, the church would never have climbed out of the place it was in to the place God wanted it to be. One of the major sections in the book *Good to Great*, written by Jim Collins deals with how vital it is to get the right people in the right places in the organization so the company can be as successful as possible.

The principles applies to ministries as well. For a church to move forward with the vision it has received, it takes the right people being given the right responsibilities. The church was ready to move forward but there needed to be some adjustments made in personnel before it could do so.

Often decisions regarding personnel within a church might create major strife in a congregation but in this case while we dealt with very serious issues, the protective hand of God was on the church. As a result, there was little fallout and nothing that hindered the forward movement of the ministry.

The right people were positioned in the right places and the church was poised for great things to happen. God had once again shown up in power and might to let everyone know that the only way things happened as they did, was because of God.

The Church Embraces the Faith Journey

To experience God interrupting your life to provide an unexpected blessing is exciting to say the least. It causes a person to want to see it happen again. It is my belief that when God's people are in a position of following Him and they are in the position that the only way they come out on the other side is by His intervention, they are living the faith journey. This church was moving ahead in faith and God was about to show them who He was in a mighty way.

As the church began to grow and parking became an issue, the property committee began to talk about the land next door to the church. They stated they had prayed for years that the church would be able to purchase the land and expand the church in a dramatic way. We went out to the property and stood on it and prayed that God would allow us to have the property. For me it was an easy call since I had seen God provide at every level. This was well within His capability. My statement after our prayer was simply why has the church not already purchased this property? I was told that they did not see how it could be paid for so they did not pursue it. All I could think of was the story of the spies who came back and said yes there are giants in the land but we are well able to overcome them. I believed God had given us that property just as He had given the Israelites the Promised Land. The people needed now to possess it. The church sought the face of God in prayer and moved in faith to purchase the property even though it appeared to stretch the church financially.

I believe God wanted to see our faith exercised so He could bless us beyond anything we could think. Not long after the land was purchased the federal government sent a letter to the church claiming imminent domain on a portion of the property close to the National Guard Armory at the far end of the property. In a heartbeat the church went from sheer delight that God had finally answered their prayer and allowed them to own the property to complete despair that they were going to lose it. Here the church faced another faith moment where they could continue to completely trust God or give in to feeling powerless.

The property had a deep ditch running through it about three-fourths of the way to the armory. The church was concerned that it was going to get the short end of the stick but as it turned out the federal government only took the quarter of the property that the church would have had difficulty using because of the ditch and in turn gave the church a sum that was enough to pay the loan on the remaining property. In actuality God did give the property to the church in a very interesting way. God's ways are not man's ways. He was glorified in the process and the people of the church were blessed and encouraged.

The more the people believed God, the more He provided. In a relatively short time the financial issues were in the past, the facilities were remodeled, additional properties had been purchased on either side of the church allowing for the future, and the church building was beginning to be filled with new people.

A Crucial Faith Decision

As had happened in the past when our church filled up, there came a faith moment and it had to be determined what the church would do to continue to reach people with the Gospel. After much prayer and deliberation the church decided to move to two Sunday Schools and remain for the time being in one worship service even though it too was filling up. In the church in South Dakota adding an additional Sunday School was not a huge undertaking but in a church of this size there was much to be done. With the space available, each Sunday School would need to be fairly close in the attendance or it would not work.

Much prayer and preparation went into the planning for the new Sunday School. Teachers were enlisted and trained, classrooms were prepared, publicity was designed, record keeping was updated, and traffic flow was finalized to allow for smooth transitions to be made from Sunday School to the Worship Service and back to another Sunday School. As the day approached there was great apprehension, however, it was all without merit. When the Sunday School attendance was tallied, the attendance in each one was within two people of the other. That would not be expected to happen even if the people were assigned a time to come. This was truly a work of God that fueled the people's vision of what could be in the future.

God continued to bless the church in every way, but that did not prevent the occasional issue from arising to challenge the direction or the process or the leadership. I was learning that in churches with longer histories there are some things that are given more importance than they deserve. For example: some people often are tied to tradition and are unyielding in their acceptance of new ideas and methodologies. Others find their security in facilities and how they have been utilized in the past. Still others are willing to accept less than the best from people in leadership. If these things are challenged there are always people who will do whatever they think is necessary to protect them whether it be godly or not. Such was the case with this church. When comfort zones were challenged reactions were both expected and anticipated.

As often happens when things move ahead on a great path, issues arose that created confusion and distractions from the true purpose of the church. Some of the issues, though hidden from plain view, were always under the surface for the remainder of the time I served as pastor. In part the issues related to how earlier issues had been addressed. When a person has a stake in the outcome of a situation and it does not go their way they will hold on to that and attempt to find retribution much later. Thankfully, many years after we had gone to another assignment, the church finally dealt with the hidden issues and moved ahead to become a great church today. Praise be to God!

The six years spent in this church represented a great time of learning for me. I found that the existing church has some dynamics that are more interwoven than in a church plant. I also found that a church plant often feels more freedom to share the Good News and take risks for the cause of Christ. The things I learned from this church could not have been learned apart from experiencing it. To see situations that were neglected for fear of uprisings and to see things left undone for lack of desire were both very hard lessons but lessons that are to be learned in virtually every existing church to some degree.

My Family Enjoyed This City

My kids were young when we moved to this church. They enjoyed their school, their friends at church, and the activities the church and community afforded them. They were old enough to understand belonging and relationships and how hard it can be to see those come to an end.

I enjoyed the opportunity to see the children interact and grow. Coaching the community baseball team and basketball team was a very special thing for me. I think all of us had put down deeper roots than we thought at the time.

During this pastorate we lived much closer to our parents and had many opportunities to spend time with them. It was good for the grandparents to spend time with our kids and see them grow up. We had been so far away in South Dakota, and their time together had been limited.

It was also during this time that my father suddenly passed away. He had come to know Jesus Christ as his personal savior late in his life, which changed our family dynamic. Before his decision for Christ we did not have a lot in common. But after his salvation experience the conversations were more about what he had read in Scripture, what his pastor had preached about, and what he had experienced on his last visit into the community to share his faith. He had truly gotten the full dose of salvation that radically changed his life. And then, he had a heart attack one day and died the next.

I was totally devastated. I could not understand why my father who had given his life to the Lord and was serving him faithfully was suddenly gone while many people that I knew to be ungodly people seemed to be doing fine.

This indeed was a faith moment for me but an extended one. I needed to have the *"why"* answered. I began to search the scriptures to find out answers to my many questions. The church members also lived through the search and study process with me and were the recipients of many sermons that dealt with the *"why"* of things.

As with other faith moments God did not leave me wondering what He was about or the *"why"* of things. I found that God does not get angry when we need to have answers to the why questions of our lives.

I learned that just because something does not make sense to me does not mean that it does not make sense at all. I found that often we find ourselves on the backside of the providential hand of God. What we see may not make sense but God sees it clearly and completely.

God let me see that because something does not make sense to me now does not mean it will never make sense. We see through a glass darkly but one day we will see things as God sees them. Just as we cannot see the picture from seeing only one puzzle piece we cannot see God's hand until more pieces of the puzzle are in place. One event in our lives does not define who we are. I may not know what this piece of the puzzle of my life means now but as more and more life experiences occur I understand more and more. It is much like the song that says, *"trials dark on every hand and we cannot understand, all the ways that God would lead us to His blessed promised land, but he'll guide us with His eye and we'll follow 'til we die, and we will understand it better by and by."* What is happening to us now may not make sense but that does not mean that it will never make sense.

Through this search, as a result of great tragedy in my life, I also learned that because something does not make sense through my earthly understanding does not mean it will not make sense when viewed through spiritual eyes and spiritual understanding. The day following my father's funeral our church was conducting revival services. I was not feeling much like going to church but I went because I was the pastor. The couple who were leading the music that week had heard of the circumstances and when they started their music before the message that day they looked over at me and said, *"Pastor, this song is for you. We believe it will be a blessing in your life."* How true that statement was then and now. The words of the song went like this, *"God is too wise to be mistaken, God is too good to be unkind, so when you don't understand, when you can't trace His hand, when you can't see His plan, trust His heart."* Wow! Those words have been very close to my heart from that moment on and when things have happened that I could not see what God was up to, I knew I needed to trust His heart.

In every faith moment of my life God has shown up and provided exactly what I needed at the time I needed it and in the quantity that I needed. I gained strength through this tragedy and through my walk with God as I searched for answers. Without that experience I would not have been prepared for the next door to open in my life and ministry.

The Time Comes to Move On

We served this church for over six years and I am sad that my time in this church was as brief as it was, but there came a time when the direction I felt my life needed to go and the direction the church wanted to go were no longer compatible. I felt the church should be involved in planting other churches and the church felt they wanted more facilities. There was no ill will or harsh feelings on my part but a sadness believing what might have been was not going to happen. To have a vision and sense that it will not be completed by you, I found to be very hard to deal with personally.

I thought about Moses and the fact that he had led the people out of Egypt and on the road to the Promised Land, but when the time came to enter in he was not the one to take those final steps. Indeed, it is a hard thing to handle.

So what would God do with me and my family now? I had served ten years as a church planter and six years as a pastor of a great church with much potential. I had learned many things from experience and had been able to get my Seminary degree while pastoring the Oklahoma church. What happened next was something none of us could have predicted or expected. Our lives and ministry were about to take a dramatic twist that would take us on yet another exciting adventure.

I had always assumed that a call to ministry meant that I would pastor a church all my life. I had been a pastor for over 16 years at this point and did not expect things to change but change they did.

After a short time in the mountains of Arizona pastoring a church where they needed to complete their facilities as well as the documentation that would allow them to be more effective, God completely shifted my gears and led me in a path I never expected.

Although it was a brief two year stay in the church in Northern Arizona, I learned much about being a pastor where the people loved us dearly and treated us better and with more kindness than any place we had served before. The scenery was nice, the church was beautiful, the people were wonderful but it was not intended for us to be there long-term. We were not sure what God had in store, but somehow we knew it was not what we were doing.

✝ CHAPTER SIX
A Complete Shift in Direction

I was asked to consider becoming the Director of Missions for the Central Association of Southern Baptists in Phoenix, Arizona. I had no real idea what a Director of Missions did, much less what I would do if called.

Pam and I talked and prayed to seek God's direction for our lives. This was something completely new and in a ministry field I knew nothing about. God had blessed my time as a pastor and church planter greatly. Why would I want to do anything else? That was the question we were wrestling with so intently. God had always given both of us His peace and His direction for our lives so we were confident He would show us clearly what He wanted us to do.

Once again God was faithful and began to clearly make His will known for our lives. What we were about to do made very little sense as man would determine but it made sense to us because we knew it was what God wanted for us. From the time we began our ministry by moving sight unseen to South Dakota our lives had been one faith adventure after another. For some reason God had not allowed us to become comfortable in any role He called us to fulfill. As we would see in later years God has held true to His pattern and given us an incredibly exciting adventure. The common thread has been that our passion is seeing new churches come to life and grow to maturity and reproduce. Little did I know that the role I was taking on in Phoenix would accentuate that passion even more.

We found ourselves back in a place where we were totally dependent upon the provision and protection of God. Not knowing the field of ministry I was about to enter caused me to seek the face of God for vision and direction.

God put some things in my mind and I started to put them on paper to share with the search team. When I finished writing what I would share with them it was four pages long and contained what I believed an Association should look like, how it should function, and the steps to take to move to that structure. The paper also did not describe any Association I was familiar with anywhere in the country. I was not surprised.

Not only was I embarking on a path I had never taken in a field I had never served but I was now proposing a function and structure no one had ever seen. I was not sure if the search team would accept this position paper or not. They could easily have determined that they wanted to keep the Association pretty much as it had been for many years. This proposal was clearly different and had some inherent risk to it. The decision of the search team was crucial because had they chosen to keep things as they were I could not have accepted the position. Fortunately, they were ready and willing to try something new if it meant the Association of churches would have an impact on the ability of churches to fulfill their vision.

A New Path is Chosen

The search team was confident that I was the person they wanted to recommend to the Executive Board for a vote. They assured me that this was going to be a breeze and the vote was a mere formality. I was not so sure. I recalled the fact that the person that was recommended before me was voted down by the Executive Board and did not receive the call to come. I was certain the search team told them the same thing.

As Pam and I waited in a back room of the church where the meeting was held we were filled with conflicting feelings and emotions. We were excited about moving to Phoenix, a city with an almost mysterious draw for people. We were excited about the great possibilities to see the vision God had given me become reality. At the same time we were uneasy about taking a role I had never done before.

Our lives had been up to this point filled with faith moments that shaped who we were and what we were. We knew instinctively that God would take care of us and that with the call comes the ability to fulfill that call. All of that sounds wonderful but when you are about to enter the unknown, you instinctively question why am I doing this?

Fortunately we did not have to wait long and when we were brought back into the room we were told the vote was 100% in favor of me taking this new role. The search team asked us if we felt God would have us take this position to which we replied yes.

Time to Get Started

I became the Director of Missions in Phoenix, Arizona with a fresh mandate and a clear and compelling vision to fulfill. As I had observed Associations in the past they were predominantly geared toward fellowship and offered training and other things churches might need. These training opportunities were announced to the churches and generally conducted at the Associational building by Associational staff.

In the era when information was disseminated through denominational channels, the Association being one of them, this model worked very well. The latest and greatest training and other opportunities were sent through the pipeline and conducted in the Associations. Churches were accustomed to sending their members to these training and fellowship opportunities so the Associations had well defined parameters to follow.

During the time I became a Director of Missions there was a paradigm shift occurring in the technology world. The internet had made information accessible to almost everyone at the touch of a button. No longer did churches and church members need to wait for the information to work its way through the pipeline of denominational channels. The information was readily available. The Association that still believed it's role was to disseminate information was quickly becoming obsolete. Attendance at Associational activities and training events began to wane and finances from churches began to decline. This was not just an isolated occurrence: it was becoming the norm.

As I took stock of where this Association stood structurally and functionally it was a typical Association that had done well for years but was now on hold. The Association had staff to carry out programs and ministries. It had a building where training meetings had occurred for years. It had a budget that was static and used primarily for Associational stability. There was little available for the churches. This is not an indictment of the Association. It had been very successful in doing things for years but the entire landscape had changed.

As Pam and I prayed we knew this was going to be at least as great a challenge as planting a church or seeing a church turn around. This Association had an even longer history than the Oklahoma church where I had pastored. I learned there that people become very attached to things, even when they are no longer functioning or needed. This would take all of our lessons learned if the vision presented was to become reality. This certainly was going to be a faith venture.

New Wine in New Wine Skins

Scripture tells us that to put new wine in old wineskins will cause the destruction of both the wineskin and the wine. If there is to be new wine there must also be accompanying new wineskins. After gaining the support for this new vision the most difficult aspect was going to be the establishment of new structures to carry out the vision.

One of the first things I did after becoming the Director of Missions was to contact a friend in California who had been a Director of Missions for many years and had been very successful. I wanted to learn from him what this new role involved and what I needed to know to become as effective as possible.

He shared with me out of his wealth of experience and told me of a group of Directors of Missions that met regularly to learn from one another and see how they could better serve their churches. This was an invitation only meeting but he said he would ask them if I could join them when they met again. I was accepted into this group and quickly learned that these were very skilled and capable men who were not following the traditional model of Associational life and structure. They were creative thinkers who critiqued each other firmly but lovingly and provided accountability for each other. I quickly saw how I fit into this group and that my vision for the Association was not like theirs but was an acceptable model for all to gain from. These men helped to shape my thinking as a Director of Missions and helped me gain the confidence I needed to fulfill this very different role.

Shortly after meeting with my friend in California I asked him to come to Phoenix and meet with our key leaders to help us design a strategic plan to begin to implement the new vision. Realizing this new vision could not fit into the old structures, we decided to start by thinking about the type of structure that would allow the new vision to flow freely and unobstructed.

The vision God had given to me was radically different than what any Association had undertaken. I believed that the Association existed to strengthen and support the vision of the local church rather than the churches supporting Associational ministries. In the current structure there were committees, staff, buildings, benevolence ministries and a host of other *"church type"* things the Association was attempting to do. As a result, there were limited resources available for the churches and the vision God had given them.

Having dealt with long-standing ministries and the strong feelings and attachments people have to them in my Oklahoma church, I knew the implementation of the vision would be like maneuvering a ship through a mine field. Every decision that would be made from that point forward would need to be tempered by the potential ramifications on the overall direction of the Association.

As my wife Pam could attest, patience and longsuffering did not rank very high on my spiritual gift list. Life to me is pretty much black and white with few departures from that model. For me to be involved in the transformation of an organization in a ministry field with which I was unfamiliar and which required great patience and longsuffering was a clear indicator that God really does have a sense of humor. This was another great faith moment for me. I was in a place that was far from my comfort zone and at a point that if God did not take the helm and steer this ship I would be in serious trouble.

Throughout my ministry God had always shown up when I needed Him the most. This was no exception. As the strategy development began with the key leaders of the Association they sensed the same leading from God that I had sensed. The direction they wanted to go was exactly the direction I wanted to go. For the several days we spent praying, thinking, strategizing, and developing a strategic process, God was walking ahead of us and showing us the path to take at every crossroad.

The New Association is Born

After much prayer and hard work the time had come to reveal what the new Association would look like for the future. The *"bones"* of the organization were about to be seen for the first time. This was a very exciting moment that was filled with great anticipation and a twinge of fear. How would this be received by all the members of the Executive Board? Would the leadership and pastors actually embrace this foreign concept? We were all about to find out.

The Association would focus on three basic avenues of service to the churches. The first was leadership development. Pastors and leaders would have the opportunity to receive training they felt they needed when they felt they needed it. No longer would the training be a broad stroke where everyone could come and maybe a few would receive some benefit. This process asked the leadership of the church to detail how the training would assist them in achieving their vision and estimate the cost. The church's leadership would also recommend the best training opportunity. Once the type of training was determined and the cost and location were set, the Association would determine what portion of the cost the Association would bear. By working this way, the leadership received assistance at the most critical point of their need and the Association was released from the obligation of duplicating trainings it could never reproduce.

The second area the Association would focus on was strengthening existing churches. The Association saw the need for healthy and strong churches to do the work of God. Churches would be able to make a request for the Association to assist them with evangelism and staff opportunities that they could not fund entirely on their own. The Association was willing to work with any church to help them achieve their vision. With each request, the church was required to detail what the event or activity was, how it fit within the framework of the vision of the church, what the church expected God to do, what the cost of the event or activity was along with the church's contribution, and finally what their plan for follow-up entailed. This would not turn the Association into a money machine but would help pastors and church leaders move through the planning process and understand that each event or activity was not simply a random event but was part of a continuous plan that was moving the church toward accomplishing their vision. No longer would the Association spoon-feed the churches with programs that did not fit their situation. Each church would need to pray and plan together to determine where they were, where they wanted to go, and how they would get there.

The third aspect the Association would focus on was assisting churches to plant new, strong, healthy, reproducing churches. In the context of the Association and the Phoenix metropolitan area, church planting would consume a large amount of the Association's budget over the next several years. There was such a need and the churches in the area were losing ground as new communities were being developed without a church presence inside the boundaries. Creating these partnerships would prove to be the avenue for seeing new churches birthed in strength not in survival.

The presentation of what the new Association would look like and what it would do seemed very simple and straight forward. It all could be boiled down to the phrase, *"healthy pastors grow healthy churches that have healthy babies on purpose."* The concept seems basic, but it required a lot of change from the way things had been.

We could assist the churches in carrying out their unique vision and without adding a staff position for every circumstance. In fact, in this structure less staff could handle the work and the need for a building for everyone to gather in was no longer there. Invariably, each church would have different struggles, different ministries, and different needs. The plan allowed the Association to dynamically adjust to each situation.

The presentation was received wholeheartedly and without many, if any, questions. Everyone was for it and left the meeting excited. However, I realized that people will vote for something with their pencils and not really vote for it with their heart. The responsibility rested with the churches and not the Association, which required a cultural change. This took a great deal of time and patience, which seemed to be the biggest thing God was working on in my life.

Making the transition from a traditional committee structure where the Executive Board wielded the power to a team-based structure where the teams were empowered to make the day to day decisions, develop the budget, and expend funds was accomplished by running dual tracks. There were still committees in place (most of which did not meet the previous year for any reason) but at the same time the teams began to engage the churches in the new model. It was not long before the churches realized that the Association was serious about helping them. Momentum built for the new model and the old structure seemed to be fading into the distance. The interesting thing was that no one really seemed to mind that the old way was quickly fading.

The Rubber Hits the Road

As much as everyone believed in the new process, the one thing lacking was the resources to do what was being promised. For several years the Association had survived on funds that did not cover much more than its own operating expenses. There needed to be an infusion of resources to allow the Association to begin to implement the new structure. This would prove to be one of the first of many big faith moments experienced over the next ten years.

The option of selling the Associational building was presented with the suggestion to invest the money and use the interest to begin to resource the vision of the churches. It is of note that the Association owned the building outright and that it had been built by people from the churches twenty-five years earlier. I know people well enough to know that there were some people within the churches of the Association that were heavily invested with their hearts in the Associational building. Anything that might affect it would be of great interest to them.

As the time came for the vote there was actually little discussion from the crowd. The greatest concern expressed was for the staff members who were used to meeting there. It was explained that the Association would still maintain offices but in a local church and that the current staff was fine with the move if it helped the Association move toward the new vision. What could have been an extremely explosive topic turned out to be a time when more of the people and churches were galvanized to move ahead together toward the resourcing model. God certainly had shown up in a mighty way to orchestrate the meeting, the presentation, and the vote, so that all was accomplished and the people were brought together.

On the Home Front

While all was moving at a frantic pace at the office with the sale of the building, establishing relationships, and spreading the vision, our family was trying to get settled into the Phoenix area. After extensive searching we bought a house in the northwest part of the Valley of the Sun in a community called Glendale. The housing development we moved into was the last housing development on the north side of the city. All that lay to the north was cactus and coyotes.

Having found a house, we were on the lookout for a church where we could get involved and where our children could have some friends and be in a youth group. We looked around and tried several churches which allowed me to meet more pastors and see their work. Nothing seemed to fit. We were concerned that there was not a church in the vicinity of our home. This was a big decision for our family.

The next week at the office I had a meeting with three men who were pastors in the Association who were forming a partnership to investigate the possibility of starting a new church in the northwest part of the city. When they mentioned the location, I told them that is where my family and I lived. At that moment I knew that we were going to be part of that new church. It seemed odd to some that we would place our children in a new church where they would be the only youth and not have an established youth group to join. This would also be the first time they would be in a church where their dad was not the pastor. My wife and I had been church planters and knew how much work was involved and our children had been involved with every aspect of our faith journey up to this point, but none of us expressed hesitation to jump in and help this new church grow. We all prayed about it and everyone felt that helping start this new church was what we were supposed to do. Pam and I had a life-changing church planting experience in South Dakota; this new church would prove to be a life-changing church planting experience for our teenagers.

The First New Church is Born

I had not been part of a church plant through a partnership before, but I was a willing learner. I had only seen a person step out and dig the new church out of the ground and trust God for the needs, or a single church willing to sponsor a new location. In this process, local churches, along with the State Convention and Association would provide a network of support and strength for the new church.

The general location for the new church was determined but the logistics were not yet in place for the actual starting place and a permanent location. After much prayer and negotiation the new church began to meet in the community room of the local fire station. This was a small room with a capacity of fifty people. The sign on the wall stated fifty people was the maximum number of people allowed and the fire marshal was just around the corner so the number would need to be adhered to very closely.

One of the churches in the partnership determined that the church would purchase five acres of land just north of the proposed meeting site. So it appeared every thing was coming together to see the new church start. What was needed then was the right person to become the pastor of the new church.

The Search for the New Pastor Begins

The churches making up the partnership formed a pastor search team and allowed me to meet with them since at that point my family was the new church. Resumes were sought and many were received. The team prayed over them but there was not a clear indication to all involved who was to be the new pastor. I asked them if I could speak to a person I had attended seminary with a few years before. He was younger than me and was a great communicator and someone everyone liked to be around. They said that I should contact him to see if he was interested.

He was pastor of a church in Oklahoma at the time and I honestly did not know how he would feel about moving to Arizona and starting a new church. His family and his wife's family lived near where he was currently serving and he had two little girls in preschool.

When I shared with him the reason I had called he was immediately excited and shared with me his heart for what he sensed God was doing in his life. The bottom line was that he would send a resume for us to consider.

When the others on the search team read the resume they were in agreement that he should be extended a call to serve as pastor of the new church that would start with his family and my family. This was a faith moment for me as I thought about and prayed about the person who would be the pastor to my family for the next decade. Having peace about it, the call was made and he accepted.

While our new pastor and his family were making their way to Arizona, the partnership was busy securing the temporary meeting site and finalizing the loan to purchase the five acres. The week he arrived and became pastor of the new church the loan was secured and the land purchase was complete. This, as it turned out, was also a faith moment. Property was purchased and construction of a new building would soon begin that would eventually become the new church's responsibility, and at that time, the new church was the pastor's family and my family. That was an overwhelming feeling and we relied on our faith to prevent us from panicking. This was church planting on a different level.

Shortly after the pastor arrived, the new church held its first service in the fire station community room with 32 people in attendance. Everyone was excited. The new church was off and running. Each week there would be new faces and an air of expectancy.

For Pam and I this was not new. It reminded us of South Dakota where there was great excitement as the people would gather for worship and the study of God's Word. For our teenagers, Adam and Amy, this was a brand new experience. They were very young in South Dakota and the church was already built before they were born. Here, they were able to see and experience the birth of a church. Preparation for the services started early as Adam would load the keyboard from our house into his pick-up truck and haul it to the church site. Amy would be there with a broom in her hand sweeping out the crickets that had accumulated over the last week. Pam arrived early to prepare the music, and then play the keyboard for the service. Everyone had a role to play. When I was there I would serve as a greeter and an usher. Often I would be ministering in one of the other churches in the Association but I was in my church as often as possible.

The Association Gets an Infusion of Resources

Our new church was off the ground and doing well. It was the first of many new churches that would be birthed over the next ten years. The Association had been restructured and relocated and had implemented the new strategy to the degree it could with the resources available. The financial giving to the Association was beginning to show signs of improvement, churches were being blessed, and money was being saved by moving the Associational offices to a church facility.

At this time the North American Mission Board contacted me about a program called *Mega Focus* they had been using with Associations in cities of one million or more. It was a strategic development process that allowed an Association to hear from churches how they would prioritize their needs. Once priorities were determined, the North American Mission Board would provide significant resources to carry out the plan.

We had worked through the process of establishing our churches' priorities but still did not have the resources to fully operate our system. I saw this as an opportunity to galvanize support for the direction the Association was moving and infuse the work with some much-needed resources. I contacted the North American Mission Board and told them we were interested.

Not long after, a representative from the North American Mission Board came to Phoenix to meet with our key leaders and present how the process would work. We had a choice of who might help us with the process and we chose our friend from California since he already knew us and our leaders trusted him.

The *Mega Focus* process was both a preparation process and an implementation process. For several months we heard from the churches what each one felt they needed. Once the information was gathered, plans and projects were put into motion to allocate the resources that were set to come from the North American Mission Board. Morale was high and churches were excited. When the time came for the implementation phase, due to some upheaval at the North American Mission Board, the amount the Association received was only half of what was expected. After the initial shock passed, we took stock of where we were and what we did have and were thankful to the Lord for what He had provided.

The *Mega Focus* turned out to be a wonderful experience for the Association and the churches that were involved. Individual churches were able to do projects they would not otherwise have been able to do. As they grew and worked together they became stronger and more capable of fulfilling their vision without much outside assistance. Another benefit of this process was that the financial giving by the churches to the Association grew because they saw relevance in what the Association was doing.

The Association was able to take the resources from the North American Mission Board and utilize them in the church planting efforts that were in the planning stages. I was beginning to learn how church planting could be done effectively and see them started in a mode of strength, not survival. The *Mega Focus* process provided clarity of direction and purpose and enough of a surge in resources to begin to move the organization towards its vision.

More Family Time

After Mega Focus there was an extended period where God blessed our lives personally and He also blessed the Association. For us, we enjoyed our new home. The scenery was beautiful, it was peaceful, and it was only two miles from where the new church was being built. We enjoyed our new city. Phoenix is an amazing place to live.

We could understand the mystique that seemed to surround the city. Adam and I enjoyed getting to play golf together on some of the most beautiful golf courses on the planet. Pam and Amy were able to visit some amazing shopping malls and museums. We enjoyed our new church. It was fun, exciting, energetic, and growing. We enjoyed each other. This was a wonderful time of refreshment and newness in our lives and our spirit. We were thankful to God for what He had done in our lives and His favor to bring us to a place where each of us could find fulfillment.

One of the things we had all agreed to as a family was that we were going to spend more time doing things together than we had when I was pastoring. I had always been a workaholic. The church came first more often than not. I did not realize the effect that had on our family life because I felt I was doing the right thing. I had come to realize how wrong I had been all those years. I had neglected the very people I loved the most. I was determined to do things differently.

In my new role the pressures of constant availability were not there. I was able to come home and actually relax rather than always feeling there was something else I needed to do. There was just as much work to do as before but my attitude was different. How I viewed my priorities had changed.

Each church was independent and my role was to resource their vision. It was fast-paced and stressful but it was very rewarding. As churches were blessed and strengthened I felt a great sense of satisfaction and joy. I still preached often in various churches, but my focus was on how to assist the churches in the Association to be as effective as possible.

During this season of blessing the finances of the Association took a dramatic turn upward. New churches were being started stronger with the additional support available. I was living out my calling within the framework of the Association as new churches began to dot the landscape where there were none before.

The structure established in the early days was working as envisioned and pastors and leaders had bought in to the system and were intricately involved. They were beginning to see the value of the Association and the role they could play and were beginning to *"own"* the ministry.

† CHAPTER SEVEN
The Associational Model is Noticed

The group of Directors of Missions which I had joined, periodically came together to learn from one another. In one of those meetings I was asked to explain how the structure of our Association worked and how our new churches were being started so effectively. Our structure was unique to our Association at this point and they were curious. They noticed that the churches being started in our Association seemed able to move past many of the barriers to growth, secure their facilities and become self-sustaining much more quickly than in other places. Because of what was happening in our Association, they wanted to investigate and see if they could better serve their churches.

I began the explanation by telling them the philosophy of the Association was simply that everything was done to help the local church be as successful as possible in fulfilling its mission. That sounds oversimplified but that was the key to all that took place within the Associational structure. I also told them that churches must be started in strength rather than in a survival mode. It did not matter how many were started. What did matter was how many grew up healthy, strong, and able to reproduce. The model and process we were using was unique but in its infancy at the time. This process with many revisions and updates would ultimately become the *Count the Cost* process. I commend the churches in Arizona that were willing to make this their church planting process. By doing, so they have paved the way for churches today to become stronger and healthier much faster.

I believed the pastors and churches were on the frontlines in the spiritual battle being waged for the souls of men, women, boys, and girls. They were, as fighter pilots call themselves, the *"pointy end of the spear."* They were the first into the battle.

The Association, and for that matter the State Conventions, National Conventions and all Para-Church organizations are behind the lines and should be asking one simple question, *"Is everything we do contributing to the success of this mission?"* The Association and the other entities are not the pointy end of the spear and have a completely different role to play. Difficulties arise and effectiveness diminishes when all parties attempt to be the church and assume the role never intended for them.

Our Association knew its role and was determined to fulfill that role as effectively as possible by supplying what the churches needed when they needed it so they could carry out their mission.

Less is More

In order for the Association to fulfill its role it had to focus on what it was going to do, but equally important was to focus on what it was not going to do. This is when I told the group of Directors of Missions that this was a huge faith moment for me. I am fairly comfortable with establishing something new but I find it more difficult to remove things that seem fine to everyone else. As it turns out, I am not alone in this struggle. Determining what will not be done is the most neglected aspect of leadership that I have witnessed in my years of service.

I went on to share that the Association had many committees and several ministry points. When determining what the Association would do and what it would not do, these ministry points also had to be considered. One question was asked repeatedly as we narrowed our focus, *"Is this an Associational responsibility or a church responsibility?"* We discovered that the Association had usurped many of the ministries that churches do. It was not acting in the supportive role but was attempting to be the *"pointy end of the spear"* and encroaching on the church's role. For example, many Associations attempt to start churches rather than churches starting churches. To some this may sound like semantics but the reality is that the baby grows up to look like the parent in most cases. In my family's case our children were fortunate and grew up looking like their mother.

The Association owned and operated a food and clothing distribution center in the inner city for many years. Through this process it was determined that churches could handle benevolence situations much better than an Association could since the Association had no manpower other than what churches provide.

While the Association transitioned out of the administrative role at the food distribution center, it provided a place for a new church to be started in the facility and the food and clothing distribution became an evangelism and ministry aspect of their vision. The new church had the people and passion to impact people's lives. The Association resourced the new church, allowing them to have the money to carry out this needed ministry. The Association and the church were now in their respective roles and God's blessings continue to flow through that church today.

As the Association clarified what it would do and what it would not do, priorities emerged. Teams were established to address three critical priorities: Leadership Development, Church Strengthening and Church Planting. Though we listed these as our three priorities, they did not hold equal weight. Church planting was the critical need in our city so church planting became the driving force of the work. Assisting churches that desired to plant new churches fit right into my call and passion. Our Association had streamlined its focus and began using teams rather than committees to complete the work.

Functional Changes

Committees gather data, investigate possibilities, and report their findings and recommendations to another body for approval and implementation. Given the new structure where implementation is the key, this did not seem to be the most effective and timely way for the Association to function.

On the other hand, teams gather data, investigate possibilities, develop solutions, and implement the solutions within the protocols and framework of the operation. Teams are able to take the initial concept and carry out the solution without taking it to a different body if they are given the right authority. For most people, this was a radical concept since it required a high level of trust be given to each team and did not rely on board oversight.

Each team was given the authority to develop a budget, develop operating protocols, and disburse the funds based on the church fulfilling established criteria. This empowered the people serving on the teams. The churches they came from had given the money and now they were in a position to know and determine where those resources would be best used. The churches felt more involved, more attached, more aware of what their role should be, and what they could expect from the Association.

After I had shared with the Directors of Missions they all agreed that this was something that more Associations needed to hear. Over the next several years I had the opportunity to share with other Directors of Missions in all parts of the United States about how their Association could be more effective in serving the needs of their churches.

God's Blessings Continue

During this season of God's blessing one of the highlights for me was Adam's graduation from high school. He was thinking about colleges to attend and where he might be able to get a golf scholarship. A couple of possibilities emerged so we planned a father/son senior trip. We put the golf clubs in the car and determined we would stop and play wherever we wanted to from Arizona to Oklahoma where one of the scholarship possibilities was located.

For the next ten days or so we played golf and visited potential colleges. The golf was hotly contested. Adam had become a great golfer but more than that to me, he had become a godly young man.

Also among God's blessings was the growth and development of our new church. The church had a praise band with Pam playing the keyboard and Adam learning to play the guitar. Amy and a couple of others provided vocals. The group started small but became quite skilled. The music and the pastor's personality and preaching drew people to the church.

The church had outgrown the fire station where fifty people was the maximum capacity and had moved to the atrium of the new high school just a few hundred feet south of where the new church building was being built. Every Sunday after church ended at the school, people would walk a short distance and tour the building under construction. Everyone was excited. With the atrium filling up everyone was anxious about when the new building would be completed. Each week the people could see progress.

A Public Showing of Faith... I Think?

A fairly large group was scheduled to come to work on the building and complete the roof and the inner walls but just before they came, Phoenix was deluged with rain. That caused a delay in pouring the footings and the slab, which had to be finished before the construction of the building could begin. When the crew arrived they were not able to do what they had planned to do, or so everyone thought.

It was determined that the walls and the entire roof section would be built on the ground while the slab was being completed, then hoisted into place by a huge crane. The people worked all week and were able to set the walls in place. Then came the moment of truth, the time to lift the roof section of the 15,000 square foot building and drop it into place.

Personally, I have trouble measuring for a light switch in the sheetrock. These people had built the entire roof and wall sections separately and expected them to fit together like large puzzle pieces 60 feet in the air.

Word had gotten out and the street was filled with people with their cameras. Some wanted to preserve history and I am sure some were there just in case this experiment the architect and the builders had never done before might actually work.

The crane was in place, the hooks were attached and the time came for the lift. Almost as soon as the lift started it was aborted. It was going to take a much bigger crane than anyone expected.

After another crane was secured the hooks were attached and the lift began. The roof for the 15,000 square foot building began to fly. We all held our breath as the roof moved out over the slab and the walls that would ultimately hold it up. Every measurement must be exact. After what seemed like a lifetime the roof was slowly lowered and every section was a perfect fit. We all heaved a great sigh of relief and thanked the Lord for His watchful care over us even when we did something as wild as this.

Once the roof was in place the rest of the work progressed at a normal speed and the church soon moved into the new facility. The building was designed for three phases but the church decided to build phases one and two at the same time. That was a fortunate decision because almost as quickly as the church was in the new facility it was too small and it began having multiple services.

Another Opportunity to Bless the Churches

The Association's work had become well known and respected to a large degree. In late 1998 the North American Mission Board introduced a new process to reach the largest cities in America. Phoenix was one of those cities. It was at that time one of the fastest growing cities, had a high level of intrigue and was a destination point for many people.

Many cities were being considered to attempt the first city-reaching strategy. With the structure of the Association in Phoenix utilizing partnerships and having a working relationship with the other two Associations in the surrounding municipalities and the Arizona State Convention, the North American Mission Board selected Phoenix as one of the first two cities to address the city issue.

People Were Still Wary

When the North American Mission Board came to Phoenix and shared how this new process called Strategic Focus Cities would work, there were some serious issues voiced in the meeting. Many people remembered the Mega-Focus process from years earlier and how the promised funds did not materialize. There were fears that could happen again.

Other concerns were that Atlanta, where the North American Mission Board is located, is a completely different context and culture than Arizona. The Arizonans did not want people fifteen hundred miles away dictating for them what they should be doing. These were very real and possibly partnership ending issues.

Over the course of a few meetings people began to feel more comfortable with each other and a degree of trust was established, albeit fragile. Only time would strengthen it. By the beginning of 1999 the process was underway and the city had one year to put together a strategy and an implementation plan.

The First Steps Were Key Steps

One of the first decisions made was not to try to develop a completely different structure to operate, design and implement the strategy. Each person on a team or representing a partnership, believed the churches were the key implementers and the Associations and the State Convention should serve as support for the projects and ministries that would emerge. Little did anyone know how that decision alone would set Phoenix apart from every other *Strategic Focus City*. Every other city developed a shadow organization and often the local entities were left out. Since Phoenix did not have to start over and build new relationships the process was expedited and had a greater impact.

Church planting was one of the key elements sought in the *Strategic Focus City* process. That worked well with us since church planting was the leading aspect and focus of our Association.

Another key decision was that the local arena would drive the process, not the national entity. This was a great point of contention but one that for the local churches and entities would have been a deal breaker. Fortunately at the eleventh hour the national entity agreed to the request that the local field drive the process.

Another key decision was to do everything to assist the current and ongoing vision of the local churches. This was not going to be about huge initiatives that at the end of the day were not sustainable once the national support faded.

The final key decision was finding the right person who would head up this process and lead the implementation. A search began to find the right person to lead this very important process. Several people were considered as the *Strategic Focus Cities* Coordinator. One by one they all either decided to go a different direction or the search team did not want to pursue them.

A Shot Out of the Blue

With the clock ticking and the need to find the right person who could quickly understand our local process becoming critical, a recommendation was made that shocked me and I think everyone else in the room. One of the other Directors of Missions asked me if I would consider being the Coordinator for the process. At first I dismissed the idea but as I thought about it more I remembered my initial statement to the Association I served that I would do everything I could to assist them in resourcing their vision. This could be a way for that to happen since I already knew the system and had relationships established in the field.

I told them I would check with my leadership and get back to them. The leaders were happy for me to do this but we all agreed that I would not stop being the Director of Missions to become a North American Mission Board employee. I would basically wear two hats and understand the role of each one.

Since the *Strategic Focus City* process for Phoenix was going to be through the local churches and driven by the local field this was to me a simple extension of my role as Director of Missions. Since church planting was a key element and a focus for my Association I felt this was an extension of my current role but with significantly more resources in play. I would have more people to relate to, more responsibility, and many more hours would be required. After praying with Pam and with my leaders I felt peace about it and was willing to step into the role.

Satan Ramps up His Attacks

In each of my ministries I had opposition that I understood came from Satan. At times I felt it was quite intense but I was about to find out it was nothing compared to what was ahead. The attacks began almost immediately and were not so much on me but on the people I loved. One of Satan's key attacks is to bring distress and pain on those you love to try and get you to back away from what you are supposed to do.

I received a call from my aunt in Oklahoma that my mother was taken to the hospital in serious condition and requested that I come back to be with her in what could be her last days. This was fairly sudden and I had not seen her in a while so I headed back to Oklahoma. This was one week before we were to unveil the final strategy and implementation piece for the North American Mission Board and other partners. I felt pulled in both directions.

When I arrived in Oklahoma my mother was seriously ill and had a short time left but no one knew how long. Several days into my Oklahoma trip I received a call that Pam had been in a serious car accident and was injured and could not walk.

After a few days I left Oklahoma to go home and check on Pam. She was recovering slowly but as we now know was injured much more seriously than first thought and still carries the physical reminder of the accident.

Shortly after arriving back in Phoenix I got a call from my aunt that my mother had passed away. Some in my family were unhappy that I was not there when it happened but I made the choice to attend to my wife.

When the time came for the funeral, Pam was not able to travel so I took Amy with me and went to the funeral, leaving Adam behind to help take care of his mom. This type of situation was not a one time or random occurrence. By the end of the process every person on the team had experienced devastating crises and tragedy, some more than once.

⊤ CHAPTER EIGHT
The Process is Launched

In the midst of some of the heaviest spiritual warfare I had ever been involved in the *Celebrate Jesus 2000* or *CJ2K* as we called it was launched. Excitement was high, plans were in place, partnerships were solidified and it was time to implement the plans that were developed through prayer and collaboration.

God had shown up and the process was bearing fruit in the areas of church plants, church strengthening projects, leadership training, and student ministries.

The Calm Before the Storm

It had been a time of blessing at the Association the last several years. With the added impetus of the *Strategic Focus City* process it appeared that we were in the flow of an ongoing movement of God. Many churches were started in strength, established churches were strengthened, and leaders were developed. The Associational budget was increasing and the Association had invested over $300,000 with the Baptist Foundation of Arizona, which had a spotless track record and provided high yield on investments.

With the added income from the interest on our investments, the Associational reach was growing and touching more and more churches. All seemed well. I had been the Director of Missions for almost five years and had seen God bless beyond my expectations and the extra income allowed the Association to have a significant monetary reserve.

Personally, we were in the best shape of our lives financially and had placed college fund money in the Baptist Foundation of Arizona to be used when our son would start college in just a few months.

And then, the unthinkable happened. An event no one could foresee would shake the core of everything that was underway. The Association would be put at risk. The church plants that were in very fragile stages would be put at risk. Our personal livelihood would be put at risk.

In the midst of the greatest blessing came the greatest challenge to everything we had worked on for the past five years. The spiritual warfare was about to take an exponential surge that would catch everyone off guard. This was going to be one of the most critical faith moments I had faced up to that point.

The Unexpected Happens

The Baptist Foundation of Arizona had been an integral part of the Arizona Southern Baptist Convention for almost fifty years and had been a trusted and true friend of churches during that time. When it was announced that the Baptist Foundation of Arizona was shutting down, it came as a shock to everyone. It was a time when people were afraid and not sure what to do.

On many levels there were questions that needed answers but for what seemed like an eternity there were no answers. In the *Strategic Focus City* process the discussion centered on: what now? Could an effective process be conducted in a city where one of the key Baptist entities was now in legal trouble that, as it would turn out, would have an effect on thousands of individuals and churches across the nation?

For the Association, the discussion was based on the loss of the funds that were deposited with the Foundation. Over $300,000 was on deposit generating interest that was being used to support new church plants in the city. How would the Association fulfill its commitments to the new churches and survive this catastrophic loss?

Personally, the funds that were on deposit were set aside for the college education of our children which was to start that month. Our son began college the same time the Foundation closed down. We were wondering what we would do and if it was going to be possible for us to pay for his college tuition and other expenses.

There were no easy answers. Many people were devastated by the losses. The elderly in particular were hardest hit. They did not have time to rebuild their savings and they had been living on the interest of their funds. Many had to re-enter the work force at an age well past the retirement age. It was sad to watch them struggle when they did not deserve to do so.

Churches were hard hit as well. Many churches had their funds on deposit with the Baptist Foundation of Arizona for safe keeping until they would use it to build a new building or make needed renovations. One church in particular was at a point to break ground and build their new facility debt free with the funds on deposit with the Foundation. Just one week before the ground breaking the Foundation was closed and the church had to postpone their new facility and try to figure out what they would do since their money was no longer available to them. Our hearts were broken for people and churches that were at risk of not surviving because of the dealings of the Foundation.

An Unexpected Surprise Awaited Us

The situation became increasingly dire as each day passed. People's frustrations were giving way to anger. Lawsuits were filed and listed many people as defendants. Then the day came when a person came by my office and served me with papers indicating Pam and I had been named in a lawsuit related to the money lost in the Foundation.

I had never been sued before so I thought this must be a mistake. I did not work for the Foundation, had no knowledge of their operations, and had lost money personally as a result of the state shutting them down. As it turned out this was for real and I was in a position to have to defend myself for something I had nothing to do with.

My life was more than full with my family, my Association, the *Strategic Focus City* and now a lawsuit to defend. My stress level was definitely elevated. This was certainly a time when I needed God and His wisdom more than ever before. I was responsible for people and their livelihood on several levels and did not want to do anything that would put any of them at risk.

As had been my practice over the last twenty plus years of ministry I took the situation to the Lord and asked for His wisdom and guidance to see the direction to take and begin to move in that direction.

The *Strategic Focus City* process did not seem to be adversely affected by the demise of the Baptist Foundation of Arizona. Because the Foundation collapse was in the news and there was negative press toward Baptists, it was decided that the proposed large-scale media aspect of the *Strategic Focus City* process might not have been well received and those funds could be utilized in a much more effective manner. The decision that was truly from God was to take the money that would have been spent on a wide-spread media campaign and give it instead to local churches for their own publicity and media in their neighborhoods. As it turned out, the churches had established themselves as trustworthy in the neighborhoods so the Foundation's collapse did not affect their credibility. The extra local media attention on Baptists ended up being a great blessing and was utilized effectively by the churches to impact their ministry.

The Association was affected but was in a position to make the necessary adjustments to ensure the solvency and success of the churches that were being planted. These new churches were at their most fragile moment when this occurred and to be able to shield them from disaster was a blessing to them and a testament to the focus and vision of the Association. It would have been easy for the Association to have either slowed down or stopped what it was doing, but that did not happen. In fact, the Association was able to continue its progress as the new churches grew and existing churches were strengthened. Life was never the same after the fall of the Foundation but everyone learned to trust God more than before.

This was a difficult time for our family. We were attempting to cover the cost of college without any savings to do so. That meant cutting back on some things, but we were more than willing to do so for our children to get their college education. God again provided more than we could have ever expected and for the next eight years, we were able to pay for college tuition for both of our children from our regular budget, which in and of itself was a miracle of God.

The lawsuit continued for three years. It was hard to give depositions and hear people talk about you as if you were the lowest criminal in the world. I was called names and my reputation and credibility as a minister were challenged. I was offered opportunities to settle but that was not an option for me since I knew I had done nothing wrong.

After about three years of dealing with the personal lawsuit, the class action lawsuit filed on behalf of the investors who had lost money was about to be heard. I was included in that since I had lost money as an investor. I found out then that the lawyer who was to be representing me in the class action lawsuit was the same lawyer who was suing me personally. This seemed like an ethical dilemma for him and certainly unfair to me.

I informed my lawyer to approach him and tell him I was going to have him removed from the class action lawsuit over ethical compromises if the personal lawsuit was not immediately withdrawn. Since the big payout was with the class action lawsuit my suit was ended within thirty minutes. I was thankful to have it behind me.

I knew I had not been involved with anything the Foundation had done so I did not feel that I should be held accountable for their poor decisions. A huge weight had been lifted from us and we could move on with our lives.

† CHAPTER NINE

Lessons Learned from Strategic Focus Cities

The time I was involved with leading the *Strategic Focus City* process in Phoenix, Arizona was a very intense time of God's blessing, intense spiritual warfare, and personal challenges. I faced some of the greatest challenges of my ministry to that point and had seen God move in such power and might as well.

The challenges I faced drove me to the story of David the young shepherd facing the giant Goliath. I felt like I might be experiencing some of the same feelings David must have felt. How do you get your arms around a city of 3.5 million people and design a process to take the Gospel into areas that have not heard, while strengthening churches and starting new ones? A person cannot live through what my family and I had lived through without some things being implanted on their heart. I learned many things during that time that have prepared me for the work I am doing today.

Get Ready for the Fight of Your Life

I had served in what I would call some difficult places where the struggle was hard and the resources were relatively few. However, I had never been involved in a struggle of this magnitude and of this intensity in my life.

I am sure that David had never encountered such a sizable and formidable foe as Goliath. There is really no way to anticipate something like that until you find yourself in the middle of the struggle. The prayer plan that was designed and developed for the *Strategic Focus City* process was a worthy plan but, as we determined later, was not of the scale and magnitude needed to address the intensity of the struggle we faced.

It was only by the wonderful grace of God that the Phoenix *Strategic Focus City* process happened at all, much less that it made a Kingdom impact that was experienced by all who were a part of the process.

As I reflect on the awesomeness and power of God I also reflect on how small and weak each of us truly is when facing the onslaught of Satan's schemes. I learned that in every situation, whether large or small, I must be ready for the fight of my life as David was with Goliath.

Know a Giant When You See One

If we are going to fight giants it certainly helps to know one when you see one. In the story of David and Goliath, there was more fighting among the soldiers than with the giant. No one was willing to go out and face the giant but they would fight among themselves for no apparent reason.

When David showed up and was willing and ready to fight the giant there was strife among his brothers and the other soldiers. To be successful in any battle a person must be able to recognize the enemy or you will find yourself at odds with your own forces.

In Kingdom endeavors there must be a focus maintained on who the enemy really is. The enemy is not the people. The real enemy is Satan and all his forces of evil.

Do Not Believe or Respond to Criticism

Just for the record, there will be plenty of criticism to go around. David faced criticism from both the army and his own family. We should expect nothing less as we serve the Lord and challenge the gates of hell. We too will face outward criticism from the world but also from those we are closest to in our ministry.

To think that there will be no criticism for you is only deceiving yourself. Someone will always think they have a better idea of what you should be doing than you and they will not be afraid to tell you about it.

David was told he was too young to fight the giant. After all, he was not even a soldier. You will find yourself being compared to others and what they are or are not doing. Do not believe anyone else's criticism and realize you are not competing with anyone else.

In each of our individual ministries and distinctive calls from God we must be who we are and always do what we feel God is leading us to do regardless of any criticism we receive.

Realize the Giants Keep on Coming

Every day Goliath came out to challenge the army of God. If one giant is defeated it seems there is always another waiting in the wings to challenge you all over again.

During the *Strategic Focus City* process we seemed to face one giant after another. There were physical trials with sickness and death among the team members' families, myself included. There were outward assaults such as the fall of the Baptist Foundation of Arizona at a critical time in the process. There were inward trials where each member faced personal challenges and integrity challenges such as in my lawsuit. Each of these giants needed to be faced in a different way, undergirded by the power of God.

David dealt with his giant by picking up five smooth stones because he knew that this one battle was not the end of the conflict. To believe there will be a time when there is no giant to face is clearly underestimating the enemy and his resolve. Satan is in the battle for the long haul and will not quit or surrender. To be in ministry is to plan on being involved in the giant fighting business until Jesus comes.

Prepare for the Battle Well in Advance

David could face the giant because he had already faced a lion and a bear victoriously. He learned that God is able to deliver His people by His mighty hand.

David had gained the small wins (although they probably did not feel like small battles when he fought them) and was able to utilize what he had learned to face the giant with confidence. He knew that God was with him in those encounters and that God would be with him now.

As David had won small battles before facing the fight of his life, so must we who lead ministries and people be able to reference the small victories God gives us in times of great struggle.

The experiences God allows us to have builds our faith and when the crucial faith moments occur we can know that He is with us and will see us through. God builds our experience base so that when the giant shows up in our lives we are prepared.

When I was younger I taught the martial arts. Our students would learn the basics and then put them into practice in a very practical way as they defended themselves against the instructor who was not out to hurt them. As they became more skilled and more confident, they were pitted against others in the class of equal skill. During all of this sparring they were seeing what was close to "*combat-like*" conditions. Other schools around us would not have their students face off in combat-like conditions so when tournament time came, our students were, in most cases, able to defeat the other schools because our students had faced similar conditions. The students who had never faced anyone knew all the motions but lacked the confidence to succeed and were completely unprepared to carry out a plan of action.

To attempt to design, develop, and implement a Kingdom-impacting ministry of a significant magnitude without first having the knowledge that God will provide what you need on a smaller scale, is to be unprepared when the giants come.

Do Not Try to Use Someone Else's Plan

Everyone has an idea of what you need to do and what your ministry should look like. Saul tried to put his armor on David because everyone knows you must have armor to fight giants.

Regardless of the ministry God has called you to do, someone else will think they have a better idea and try to persuade you to use their method. If you do not fight well with armor then do not accept the armor of others. You must fight your fight with the gifts and talents God has supplied you with so that when there is victory He will receive the glory.

If something has worked somewhere else do not automatically assume it will work for you in your context. Your giant is unique and your method of fighting must also be unique. David would have been in trouble had he attempted to fight his giant with someone else's strategy. He knew his situation better than anyone else and so do you.

Be Strategic With Your Aim

When David fought the giant he studied him and found that there was one particular place where he was vulnerable and victory could be achieved. The stones David had picked up would only bounce off the massive and heavy armor of the giant. But, if the stone was strategically placed in the only unprotected area of the giant's forehead, he could be killed.

Each of us must be strategic as we seek to carry out God's unique calling on our life. There are many things that could be done but will they be effective and have the greatest impact on the ministry? The idea is not to see how many things can be done but rather to determine what will have the maximum impact.

All of us must be strategic with our aim. If we have only one stone we must make sure it hits the most vulnerable spot that allows us to fulfill our mission.

Utilize What You Know and Do Best

Every ministry and every calling is going to be unique and will require unique strategies, plans, and methodologies. To try to "program" your ministry would more than likely be its death knell.

Jericho was taken as a result of a unique strategy. This great walled city was very formidable and not easily penetrated. God gave Joshua a unique plan to walk around the city once per day for six days and seven times on the seventh day. I am certain there were those in the army who criticized this plan and thought they had a better one.

Because Joshua was faithful to God's plan, he led the people as God commanded and this great city fell. When it was over, God received the glory.

Goliath was defeated by a shepherd boy and a sling shot. Jericho was defeated with a marching band. These are stories of God's unique plan and strategy to defeat the enemy. No other walled cities were taken in this way and I do not know of another shepherd boy who slew a Philistine with a sling shot.

Each of us must be who we are and carry out the mission given to us in the way God tells us to or we will face defeat just as the children of Israel did at Ai when they devised their own plan and thought they were stronger without God than with Him. They were soundly defeated in their own power and strength when they should have easily prevailed on this small city.

Face Your Giants With Courage

When you find yourself in the battle of your life you can know that just as God was with David, He will be with you. David was confident and courageous because he had seen God intervene when he fought the lion and the bear and was certain God would deliver him from this uncircumcised Philistine.

We can have the same confidence and courage as David because we know that God will intercede on our behalf and when we surround ourselves with an army of prayer warriors interceding for us we will be victorious. Draw on the strength you have received from God on the occasions when you had nowhere else to turn but to Him. Just as He carried you through those difficult times, He will carry you through any current or future crisis.

Trust Your Call and His Heart

We must trust that our call into ministry is a call to listen to and obey the commands of God. We will all face hard times in our ministries when the battle will be hot, and the outlook will be dim. At those times a simple trust in God and His call will be all that you have, but here is the good news: it will be enough.

It all comes down to trusting your call and taking God at His word. In the day by day, moment by moment trials of ministry there will be times that trusting His heart will be all that you can truly count on.

Celebrate the Victory

When David defeated the giant he took the spoils to his tent where he could be continually reminded of the power and might of God. In our ministries we must find the victories we can celebrate and make much of them, always remembering the God who made them possible.

It is also important to know what victory is all about. Victory that endures is often not the flashy and visible aspects but rather in the cracks and crevices of the process. These victories are harder to see but not any less important. It could be a change in attitude that can only occur when the Spirit of God takes over. We must constantly show Satan the spoils of the battle to remind him he is a defeated foe already. A key part to any ministry strategy must be an intentional identification and magnification of the victories gained for all who are involved.

Understand You Are Not Alone

God wants us to know that He is with us throughout our ministry processes and when the victory comes (and it will) He is worthy of our praise and honor. He deserves the credit and the glory for all that is achieved.

Sometimes we feel we are alone in our service to the Lord, but we are never alone and we never accomplish eternal victories without Him. To God be the glory for the great things He has done and for what He continues to do in our lives.

† CHAPTER TEN
The Association Emerges Stronger Than Ever

Celebrate Jesus 2000, the *Strategic Focus City* initiative concluded at the end of 2000 and the follow-up was underway. This had been one of the most intense times in my life where it seemed that everything was being attacked wherever you looked. Individuals, families, organizations, churches, and other entities were all caught up in the whirlwind of that focused eighteen months.

Satan had fired his best shot and the Association, churches, and individuals were still standing. We were all bruised, battered, and tired but felt the joy and exhilaration of victory. Everyone took stock of what had been lost but also what had been gained. In most instances, things were gone, but in every instance a sense of the prevailing hand of God was present. There were definitely signs left of a great battle but the enemy had been defeated and it was time to move forward.

The Association was able, even through the crisis of financial loss, to meet all of its commitments to new church planters and to churches who were expanding their ministries. As I ponder all that happened, I realize that apart from the intercession of God all would have been lost. As it stood, the money was gone but the spirit of the churches and the people was stronger than ever. With that spirit we knew we would be able to come back from the brink stronger than ever.

Our vision was clearer and our resolve was greater than before the crisis. The new churches that were a part of that vision were growing up and increasing in size and strength. These new churches joined hearts with the other churches in the Association to ensure the giving was strong and the needs were met. Even in the greatest crisis we would face, the Lord blessed His churches and they provided record giving for what turned out to be ten years in a row.

This was a tremendous faith moment for everyone to trust God in the midst of the battle and to see His provision where there should have been no provision. We should not have been surprised by what God did for us. He has done that for centuries.

The widow with nothing but a small cruse of oil was about to be completely destitute when she looked to God for provision. The prophet Elisha told her to go out and borrow as many empty vessels as possible from her neighbors and when they are brought in, fill them with oil from her small supply. She did as she was instructed and when the vessels were brought in and she began to fill them, miraculously every vessel was filled to the brim and her oil never ran out. The woman and her sons were saved.

Another example is the feeding of the five thousand. Jesus took one small lunch brought by a boy and blessed it, broke it and gave it to the people. Five thousand were fed from just a single lunch that would not have fed a single hungry man and there were twelve baskets of food left over.

God Blesses Our Family

Our family was under attack during the previous eighteen months but God had been faithful to protect us and our children. Amy was becoming known for her art and painting skills. She had entered some local competitions and won ribbons and recognition for her work. We were extremely proud of her. She was growing up to be a beautiful young lady.

Adam was developing his musical abilities and writing songs. The praise band he was leading for the church youth group was singing and playing at events outside the church at block parties and church camps. They formed a band called *Sonburn*. I guess the title was fitting for the desert. A few years later, their band signed with a record label, they changed their name to *Stellar Kart*, won a Dove Award and had several #1 songs in the Christian music arena.

Pam was continuing to recover from the car accident she was in at the beginning of the *Strategic Focus City* process. For several weeks she was unable to walk. For her that was as painful as the physical injuries. She had always been invincible and tireless. For her to be in this condition was very strange.

When Pam could walk a little she received a walker and felt a little more of the freedom. The physical therapy was painful and at times frustrating. It was very different to see her moving slower than she usually did but it was a blessing that she was regaining her mobility.

When she gave up the walker for a cane she was able, with a little assistance, to make her way back to the keyboard to play in the praise band at church. Although she worked extremely hard in physical therapy she still carries the effects of the accident today.

It was painful to see Pam in distress but it was equally exciting to see her walk again and be able to resume most of her daily activities. I will always be grateful to God for His protection over her in the accident that could have been so much worse than it was.

I was reevaluating what it was that God wanted me to do with my life and ministry. At that time I felt God wanted me to continue to lead the Association to assist churches as they fulfilled their mission and vision. Although I was tired and a bit battered from the fray of the last couple of years I was reinvigorated to make a fresh start and move forward. New churches still needed to be started and I was thankful for the opportunity to be involved in what I knew God had called me to do.

God Adds to Our Family

When the *Strategic Focus City* process was over and the personal lawsuit was over, all of us had the opportunity to make a fresh beginning and pursue what we believed God would have for us.

It was at this time that Adam informed us that he was getting married. We were so excited. The young lady he was marrying was a beautiful young lady and such a sweetheart. You could tell they loved each other by the banter that went on between them. She loved the Lord and was a faithful follower of Jesus Christ. She was a native Phoenician with a Christian family heritage.

We could not have been more thankful than we were when Adam told us of their plans. Over the last ten plus years of their marriage we have become even more thankful that God brought them together as He did. They have loved each other and navigated the mine field of married life extremely well. I attribute that to their love for God and their love for one another.

For us, it was an answer to a prayer that Pam and I had prayed many, many times beginning before he was born that God would bring the person into his life that he could love and be loved by for the rest of their lives. Truly God answered that prayer in Sharon.

Plans Are Made for a Wedding

Once the announcement of a wedding was made it seemed that our lives were in high gear and high stress once again only this time in a joyful way. Pam was in her element helping with planning and organizing. Sharon's mother and grandmother were also right in the middle of the fray doing what mothers and grandmothers of the bride do to get ready for a wedding.

Thousands of decisions were to be made and it was clear Sharon had an amazing organizational quality that allowed her to deal with all the stresses and stay as sweet and pleasant as always.

Adam and Sharon have a love for baseball so when the time came to decide where the rehearsal dinner would take place they chose the *"Friday's"* restaurant in the upper deck of the Bank One Ballpark in downtown Phoenix. The restaurant overlooks left field and proved to be a great place for the rehearsal dinner. It was a memorable place to eat and visit with family who had traveled in for the occasion.

Planning a summer wedding in Phoenix has its challenges. Getting set up for things and not sweating to death is difficult to do. Determining what to serve at the reception is affected by the amount of heat that might be present on the day of the wedding. As it turned out, it was 116° on the wedding day. People can say it is a dry heat all they want but 116° is hot anywhere you are, wet or dry.

My Preparation for the Wedding

As a pastor I had the privilege of sharing in some of the most special moments in my children's lives. I was there when they asked Jesus to forgive them of their sins and be their Savior. I was there to baptize them after their salvation experience. Not every father has that high honor but I was fortunate to do so. Now I was in a position to perform my son's wedding.

I had done many weddings before and knew how the typical wedding went and what was usually said. However, this was not going to be a normal wedding for me, so the usual wording was not going to be sufficient.

I spent much time in prayer to determine what I might say that would indicate to them God's faithfulness to answer prayers made before they were born. We had prayed for Adam before he was born and for Sharon even though at the time we did not know her. God is a sovereign God and before time began He knew that they would be standing there together at that moment. It was not an accident. It was not chance. This was indeed a divine appointment.

I thank God that I had the wonderful privilege to share in these epic moments of both our children's lives. There is no way to place a value on being there for those moments.

Things Get Back to Normal

With the wedding behind us it was time to focus on what God wanted us to do for Him in our lives. We sensed that God wanted us to continue to share the vision of what an Association can do for the local church as it carries out its mission.

After the losses in the Baptist Foundation of Arizona the Association had to reassess its priorities and focus. It was determined that the vision and focus of the Association were to remain unchanged for the future. The teams would remain in place to develop leaders, strengthen churches, and assist churches in planting healthy and reproducing new churches.

Nothing would change. All we needed to do was to accept the financial losses and grow the Association once again. So that is what we set out to do.

In a short time God was faithful to bring about a settlement in the class action lawsuit filed on behalf of those who lost money in the Baptist Foundation of Arizona. As it turned out the investors recouped somewhere in the neighborhood of 60% of their losses. For the Association that was equal to almost $200,000. The settlement brought the Association once again to a place where it could resource the vision of its churches. The Association invested the money but not in a single investment. The investments made after the Foundation losses were much more diversified.

The giving of the churches began to increase once again so the Association was seeing larger gifts made to its ministry. The corpus of investments was increasing, resulting in the Association being able to return more to the churches to fulfill their mission.

A Serious Issue

The Association at this point had been able to place in investments about $500,000 to assist churches to do their ministry. Church planting was still a large part of what the Association was attempting to do with the churches. We all knew that new churches could grow fairly quickly if certain things were in place, but a critical issue surfaced that had the potential to shut down the church planting work.

In Phoenix the *"identity of place"* was very important to people. A church meeting in something other than a church-type facility was not given the same credibility as those who had their own facilities. Potential members seemed to desire a permanent location before they would commit to being part of a congregation.

The issue became, *"How does a new church qualify for a loan to acquire a building?"* A new church generally does not have great assets therefore it has no collateral. A new church generally does not have a great deal of cash on hand therefore it has no down payment. The offerings of a new church are generally small, so 3½ times the income will not be enough to get a loan to acquire the building. So, how does a new church overcome this seemingly hopeless issue?

A Search Begins in Earnest

The problem had been identified, now it must be overcome, but how? I began a search that would take me many places over the next two years. I visited the North American Mission Board to discuss loans for new churches. I visited banks to discuss loans for new churches.

I visited credit unions and foundations only to hear the same thing: new churches do not qualify for loans. I already had that part figured out. I knew the problem. I wanted to find someone willing to work with me to overcome the issues and help new churches grow much faster and gain self sufficiency much more quickly.

About two years into my search I met a person who was a banker and lender with his own company. As I shared with him my dilemma he began to ask questions and before long we had a fairly good understanding of what was needed.

Simply put, a lender is concerned with collateral and the ability to repay the loan. How could we keep the requirements of the lender in sight and still find a way for the new church to move ahead? It was determined that if the Association would make a deposit with his company the Association would receive interest on the deposit and the money on deposit could serve as a down payment for the new church.

Here is what happened. The Association made a deposit with the company. The Association earned interest on the deposit. When a church needed to buy land, the church did not qualify but the Association could. The company *"tagged"* 20% of the loan amount from the money on deposit from the Association and in turn made a 100% loan. By doing it this way the lender had all of our money on deposit with him, the corpus was never used which was good for us, we received an interest payment which we used to guarantee the payment, and in essence no money had changed hands. The Association was the entity taking the risks by having this money on deposit with a company, essentially acting as a bank.

Another Faith Moment Arises

Well, that gave me an answer to the dilemma of our new churches. The problem was that the Association would once again be in a position to lose everything. The Baptist Foundation was still in everyone's mind and I was not sure the Association would be willing to risk everything to help the new churches.

A special meeting was called to hear this proposal and discuss it. I had prayed that God would make the answer very clear whether we should move ahead with this proposal and risk everything or protect what we had accumulated. I knew what I believed God wanted us to do. We would soon find out whether the leadership of the Association felt the same way.

As the meeting began I shared the journey I had been on to find a way to overcome the dilemma we had that was keeping our new churches from moving forward. I shared with them the risks and told them that it was possible that the Association could once again lose everything. By this time the amount the Association had available was double what was in the Baptist Foundation of Arizona when it failed.

As I concluded my remarks I honestly did not know what to expect. I called for questions and discussion. Only one elderly person spoke. He said, *"I believe we should do it. We lost everything before and it did not kill us. I would rather we lose everything helping new churches get a solid start than have all this money and not use it to the fullest extent possible."* No one else said a word.

The vote was unanimous to move forward and in reality risk everything for the Kingdom. Again God had shown up in great power and might. What could have been a very volatile meeting was anything but volatile. The leadership in the Association was drawn together around a unifying purpose. Church planting had just taken a giant step forward. Now it was possible to secure a permanent location and provide needed facilities for new churches where before it was impossible. As a result, many great churches were started and grew up and were able to secure their future. This indeed was an exciting time and a blessing from God.

God is Pleased

After a great crisis the people of God were ready to get up, dust themselves off, and move ahead. I could not help but recall II Corinthians 4:7-10:

> *"But we have this treasure in earthen vessels, that the excellency of the power may be of God, and not of us. We are troubled on every side, yet not distressed; we are perplexed, but not in despair; persecuted, but not forsaken; cast down, but not destroyed; always bearing about in the body the dying of the Lord Jesus that the life also of Jesus might be made manifest in the body."*

That night was a watershed moment in the life of the Association. God began to bless in an even greater way. New churches were given birth in strength not in survival. Lessons were learned about church planting that are being utilized today across the nation and around the world.

The Association had many people who knew of the trials it had faced and the way it had rebounded. That gave me an opportunity to speak to many different groups around the country who wanted to know about structure and systems. They wanted to know about church planting and how you can know a church plant will be able to grow up strong. It also allowed me to meet many people that would play a part in my life and ministry years later. God was orchestrating the circumstances and preparing the way for another opportunity in ministry.

God gave us several more wonderful years of ministry in Phoenix. This period of my life taught me so many things and fostered a greater trust and a greater faith than I had known before

† CHAPTER ELEVEN
Change is in the Wind

During the last several years we spent in Phoenix God began to make some changes that would have a dramatic effect on our lives. Adam and Sharon bought a new house in north Phoenix. Adam had come to work with me at the Association as a worship consultant helping churches with their sound systems and also helping them learn how to transition into a more contemporary style of worship, as well as leading worship in some of our new church starts. Sharon was working in the Governor's office and their lives appeared pretty settled.

Sonburn, Adam's band, played weekly at our local church youth group and continued to gain a following in our state and beyond. They were playing for church block parties, concerts, youth events, and youth camps. A *Battle of the Bands* for the Southwest was held in Phoenix with five hundred bands competing for a spot in the Spirit West Coast lineup, a Christian gathering in Del Mar, California where thousands of young people gather for several days and listen to many bands on many different stages. *The Battle of the Bands* lasted three days. It was clear from the beginning that Sonburn stood head and shoulders above the other bands in the competition. I know I am biased but it was obvious.

The judges narrowed it down to three bands that would perform the next day and a winner would be chosen. Again, as the bands played *Sonburn* stole the show. We prayed the judges would see it that way and praise the Lord they did. *Sonburn* won hands down. They were off to California.

At Spirit West Coast there are many stages and side stages where bands are playing all day and into the night. *Sonburn* was given a small side stage at a time when you would not expect many people to show up but they did. They had a large crowd and everyone was excited. The boys wanted to sign with a record label and move into the Christian music business.

Not long after *Sonburn* won the *Battle of the Bands,* Adam received a call from an executive with Word Records in Nashville, Tennessee. Over the next couple of months, we watched as Adam's leadership skills emerged through the intense negotiations with the record label that ended with *Sonburn* signing a six record deal with Word Records.

One of the first things the band needed to do was to find a name that was not copywrited and one that would set them apart. Adam could probably tell this story better than I can tell it but one day at a go-cart track in California the guys settled on the name of *Stellar Kart.*

Success Means Sadness and Joy Simultaneously

Having signed with Word Records the boys in the band felt they needed to move to Nashville to be where the label was located and where the recording studios were available to them.

When the day came for them to leave it was exciting but very sad for us. It was so nice to have Adam on my staff and have Sharon close with a great job at the Governor's office. We wanted to be selfish but we knew they were making the right decision and following their dream.

Other Changes Follow

Amy had grown up so quickly and had become a beautiful young lady with a multitude of talents. She had gained recognition for her art and painting skills in a very large marketplace. She decided she would pursue the Art History career path and attend Northern Arizona University in Flagstaff, Arizona.

We were excited for her, but when the day came to load her stuff onto the truck and take her to a different city and leave her there, it was extremely difficult. The drive home was not a fun one even though the scenery was magnificent.

We were thankful that Flagstaff was not very far away and we could visit Amy and see her grow and mature. She learned a great deal about independence. She has a very strong sense of who she is and will challenge opinions and ideas that are different and do not have solid basis behind them. She had many opportunities to do just that at the fairly liberal thinking university since Amy is a very conservative young lady.

She is sweet on the outside but she is a pit bull on the inside so she would go toe to toe with people and have the information and documentation to clearly state her case. She got that from her mother. Amy, the quiet one, was a strong leader who was having the opportunity to let that aspect of her personality surface and develop.

She had the ability to take someone's position apart and they would thank her for it when it was over. Not many people can do that. At that point I did not worry much about Amy and her future. I knew she could do anything she wanted to do and hold her own with anyone. We were extremely proud of her for how she stood for her beliefs and lived what she believed.

Everything is Different Now

My ministry continued to be shaped. I had served as a church planter in the pioneer area of South Dakota where faith played such a significant role in my life. I was able to grow up and shape my theology based on experience and knowledge of God's Word. I was able to see the way God intervenes on our behalf. I had served in a turn-around church in Oklahoma where I learned more about working with people and solving problems. In this situation my faith was expanded to include things I did not experience in South Dakota and that I would need when I moved to Phoenix. I had served in the beautiful city of Phoenix in a regional capacity that again stretched my faith and my abilities. God continued to grow my faith and hone my skills.

The ministries I had the privilege of leading in the first eighteen years of ministry were so rewarding. They were not without their struggles but each of these opportunities shaped and molded me into someone far different than the person who came to town in South Dakota many years before.

At this time in our lives our world had been shaken up. Adam and Sharon had moved across the country. Amy was away at college and the dynamic of what held us together was different. What would God do next? I was not sure but I did know that circumstances and situations had brought about a different set of feelings concerning where we lived and what we would do.

What Now?

At this point in time I received a call from one of the Vice Presidents at the North American Mission Board asking if I would consider coming to the Board to lead the Associational Strategies Team. At first I had no interest in going somewhere else. The Association in Phoenix where I was serving was being blessed by God and every aspect of the work was at its pinnacle. Why would I want to consider going somewhere else and start over again in another job I knew nothing about?

As we had always done, Pam and I prayed about this possibility. We had prayed in the past and God had given answers that our friends thought would be sheer lunacy to accept. We did not know if this would be the case here or not. We loved our city, our home, our friends, our ministry, and the life God had given us there. We had weathered severe crises and saw God carry us through. Yet we knew that when God calls He always provides a way.

As I contemplated the responsibility of a national ministry I was overwhelmed. North America is a big place. I knew the attacks Satan threw at us in a regional setting and I could only imagine what they might be in a national responsibility. I wondered if I could carry out a task of that magnitude.

I thought about the ministries God had allowed me to lead and how He had always stepped up to provide for me the wisdom, tenacity, patience, and direction to carry them out. They became my lion and my bear as I thought of David. God was faithful in the Plains of South Dakota, the Midwest of Oklahoma, and the Desert of Phoenix, there was no reason He would not be faithful if He led us to the South in Georgia.

Something Unforeseen

The spiritual battle to find God's will for our lives was much more intense this time than in any of our other decisions. I was not sure what it was but it was a difficult time. I was not sure if it was me and my desire to stay where everything was comfortable and sure. I was not sure if I was concerned about leaving my daughter behind in

Arizona alone. I was not sure if possibly I was afraid to accept such a responsibility and start over. I was in my fifties then and was not sure I had another *"start over"* in me.

I weighed what Pam would feel moving away from a place we both held dear to a place we were unsure about. At my age this was a critically important decision. I could get very spiritual here and talk about Abraham picking up his family and looking for a city. I wish I could say that is how I felt but I did not feel that way. This was an agonizing time in my life and in the lives of my family.

I weighed where the Association would be without me. Inwardly I had hoped to come to the conclusion that they could not make it without me but I knew in my heart that was not true. The system that was in place was working well. The Associational staff was now only one full-time and one part-time staff member besides me. The teams were functioning and taking their responsibility seriously. I certainly was not indispensible, even if I wanted to think so.

I found myself day by day in my spirit becoming ready to accept the challenge that had been laid out before me. I had preached about John Mark returning from the mission field to his comfort and his lifestyle but always wondering what might have been going on in Antioch. I had preached that in order to be ready to move forward, the dangers and challenges of Antioch must become a stronger draw than the comforts of Jerusalem. I could have stayed in my comfortable Phoenix, but the draw of Antioch was beginning to drown out the familiar noises of Jerusalem.

A Decision is Made

After much prayer and seeking the face of God we made the decision to accept the role at the North American Mission Board. The days following were difficult days for us. We had to tell our daughter we were moving, which was very hard to do. She was in college and would stay behind. We had to tell our friends who had become so dear to us over the years that we were moving away. We had to tell our church. The pastor's family and my family had started the church and now he would be the only family left that helped start the church. He and his family were very special to us and continue to be today. We had to tell our Association. This was very hard. These were people who had trusted me when I presented things to them that made no human sense. They took care of me and cared about my family. They had arisen as a force to be reckoned with in the spiritual arena. As hard as it was to say farewell to our church in South Dakota after almost ten years, it was equally hard to say farewell to the Association after the same amount of time. The Association was not an employer, it was an extension of my family that I loved dearly. I would deeply miss them.

Next Steps

Our decision was public in the fall of 2004 and I would begin my new position January 1, 2005. There was much to do to be ready to make another transition across the country. When you have been in a place for ten years you accumulate a lot of stuff. We sat down and made a list of what needed to be done and by when. I was still working until the end of the year.

The first thing on the list was the sale of the house. This was a concern for us. Pam called the real estate person who sold us the house we were living in and asked her to come over and give us an idea of what the house might be worth and what we needed to do. She came over, loved the house and told Pam what it was worth which at that time was more than we thought. But that was not the end of the story. She said she had been working with a buyer who was looking for just this kind of house and they would probably love it.

I was in the west part of the valley showing a church planter around when Pam called. She told me what the house was worth and the real estate person had a buyer for it that day. Were we ready to sell? I told her yes. The people looked at the house at 6:00 pm and we signed the papers at 8:00 pm that day, before the For Sale sign was even in the yard.

The Lord had made a difficult concern disappear in a heartbeat. But that is not the end of the story. We told the buyers we would like to stay in the house until the end of the year and have Christmas before we left. We would be out by December 31. They said they were in no hurry to move in and gave us the opportunity to live in the house after the closing for the next two months rent-free. When God moves He moves all the way. We could now go on a house hunting trip with cash in hand. Amazing how God works!

Next on the list was another crucial decision: what do we do with the Dachshund that we have been keeping for Amy while she was at school? Amy could not take the dog to school, we had fallen in love with the dog but could not take her to Atlanta, so what were we to do? Even in the little things God is concerned. Pam met a lady with three young children who wanted a dog in the worst way. They came by to see and play with the dog and everyone had a great time. We decided to give the dog to this family. This was a traumatic and hard decision with many tears involved. Months later we asked the mother how things were going with the dog. She said everyone had fallen in love with the dog, especially her. The boys got to play with the dog but it had adopted her and she had adopted it. Again God's provision was great.

Another key decision was determining where we would live in Georgia. In late October we took a trip to Atlanta to see the area, meet people at the North American Mission Board and get a feel for where we might want to live.

We were in Atlanta for five days and it rained each of the five days. This was quite different than the weather we experienced in Phoenix. Little did I realize how much it rains in Atlanta. However, it was pretty with the leaves changing and a nip in the air.

I had never been to the North American Mission Board before and I felt a little anxious. It is located in Alpharetta which is a suburb of Atlanta in a very nice area of the city. The building itself was a little overwhelming at first. It was a large acreage with a small lake and a five story complex of offices and conference rooms. As we went inside we were met by some friends we knew from earlier days who had gone to work there.

The Vice President who had hired me had told me only a week before that he would be leaving the Board the last of December and would not be working with me after all. That was a shock and a cause for us to rethink our choice to leave where we were. We had already sold our house but the key issue for us was whether or not God was calling us here. After praying about the situation we sensed that God was leading us there whether the person who asked us to come was there or not. That was another faith moment for us.

I found my future office on the fifth floor in the northwest corner. I met the staff I would be leading and enjoyed the brief visit we had together. My coming was shaking things up from their status quo and I wanted to be sensitive to any apprehension they might be feeling.

Finding a House

Pam had researched the area and had a pretty good idea of where we wanted to start looking for a home. Part of the issue was the driving time from where we would live to the Board. It seemed no matter where or in which direction, whether eight miles or eighteen miles, it would take at least forty-five minutes to get there. Traffic would definitely be an issue.

The first few houses were a real wake up call for us. The housing market was still good at that time and the amount of house we could get for the money was going to be less than we thought. To get what we felt we needed to get would require us to expand our price range. To do so would require us to make some shifts in other areas.

After searching several locations we finally found the house we liked in an area we liked. The problem is that it was priced beyond our range. After discussing it we decided to make the offer and trust God with the rest. The seller accepted the offer and we had a place to move to when the time came. Ultimately we would get the house and much of the furniture since the seller was needing funds to close. It turned out to be a win for the seller and for us.

Finishing Strong

After we returned from Georgia to Arizona we set our sights on finishing well. The Association had been good to us and we wanted to leave well. As it turned out, one of the properties we had purchased earlier in our ministry was sold just before we left and the sale allowed the Association to add $250,000 to the investment base. I felt pretty good when the funds were deposited.

Whether we were ready or not, the time came for us to prepare to leave Arizona. Before we left the Association hosted a going away party for us to celebrate the ministry we had all shared. Many people shared from their heart and said very nice things that blessed us greatly. I learned so much during this time in my ministry, and they learned right along with me.

I am not much of a party person but this was needed for them and for us. I will always have a place in my heart for Phoenix and the wonderful pastors and churches I had the privilege to labor with for so many years. Regardless of what the future would hold this would be a cherished time in our lives.

✝ CHAPTER TWELVE
The Faith Journey Continues

With the Phoenix chapter closed we turned our attention to the new responsibility at the North American Mission Board. My ministry began in a small community in a very small church, moved to a metropolitan area with a fairly large church, transitioned into a regional responsibility in a very large city, and was transitioning again to a national responsibility in a denominational capacity.

My new role would make me responsible for equipping the Directors of Missions for more than twelve hundred Associations of churches across North America. The scenario seemed familiar to me by now. Start from scratch in an unfamiliar field, see the need, then make the necessary changes to transition the process to be more effective. Church planting, my underlying passion in all aspects of ministry, was also a vital aspect of this new assignment.

But Wait... Surprise!

We had barely settled in to our new house and our new role when the telephone rang and a young gentlemen on the other end of the line asked if he could talk with me. He sounded a little nervous and I had a feeling I knew what he was going to ask, and yes, that was it. He asked for our daughter's hand in marriage. I think he must have waited until we moved 1700 miles across the country so he could do it over the phone instead of braving the face to face discussion. After asking the proper fatherly questions and making him answer to my satisfaction, I gave him my blessing. Then I made him talk to Pam!

So now we had a long-distance wedding to plan. I say *"we,"* but this was really mom and daughter collaboration. Us guys just do as we are told when it comes to these things. The phones were busy for the next several months with a few Atlanta to Phoenix trips thrown in for good measure. The bride and the wedding were beautiful and all went well. I was honored to have the opportunity to speak into Amy and T.J.'s marriage at their ceremony. It was such a blessing to be a part of that life-changing moment in their lives.

We are thankful to God for the husband he provided for our daughter and are so grateful that they both have a heart for God and are serving Him together.

Back to Work

Associations have celebrated over 300 years of service, and in that time their role has changed several times. In the early days the Association consisted of churches scattered over a geographic region desiring fellowship and commonality of mission and purpose. To achieve this goal the churches formed the Association to foster fellowship and to be a centralized agency for missions.

The churches were fairly small and the Association provided them an avenue to be part of something larger than themselves. The Association also provided resources pooled together by the churches to assist any particular church with a pressing need or a ministry opportunity. By providing these services the Association played a vital role in the expansion and growth of the churches.

Transforming the Role of Associations

As time went by the Southern Baptist Convention grew and as it did so other entities were formed to assist the churches in fulfilling their desire to share the Gospel with the whole world. State Conventions were formed and over time became the mission agency the churches relied upon for their information and training. As these conventions became stronger the Associations faced an identity crisis.

Even more striking than the emergence of the State Conventions was the move by many of the Associations to seemingly take on the role of the church. Associations began to structure themselves like churches even to the point of electing an Associational pianist. If a person looked at an Associational annual report they would not be able to discern if it was for a church or an Association. Just as the State Conventions had become the entity charged with missions, the Associations were feeling charged with the ministries that normally were done by churches. The challenge for roles was intense. Directors of Missions functioned more like pastors than they did consultants or coaches or even cheerleaders. Associations began to own ministries that had been church ministries in the past such as benevolence and feeding the hungry. Although these are noble ministries and should be carried out, the Association is not structured for follow up like a church. As a result, success was determined by the amount of activity rather than the results that activity produced.

The Challenge is Accepted

Having served as a Director of Missions in an Association that was drastically different than that which is described above, the challenge was to convince people on a national scale that there was a better way for Associations to function. I knew the Association as it was functioning was not in a position to carry out the purpose for which it was created. A new focus needed to be shared and accepted to change the culture of the Association from the inside out.

My first decision was to seek God as to what my role was to be in this challenge. I called my team together and we identified what was currently happening in Associations across North America. We noted the successes and we also noted the shortcomings of the current Associational operations. Once we identified the issues we were facing we turned our attention to the things we could initiate that would begin to change the culture of Associations and refocus them on their main purpose.

The most recurring issue was that Associations were not doing what they were designed to do. In almost every Associational document there is the statement that it exists to either strengthen, assist, resource or care for the churches. Upon examination, the functions and programs of the Associations in many cases were determined to be doing the exact opposite. The Associations had established their ministries and were asking the churches to provide people and money to carry them out. Shockingly, in most Associations there was no budget money to assist or help any churches. In fact the Associations seemed to be in competition with churches for the manpower and money that was available. Obviously, this is not how it was designed to function.

The Work Begins to Change a Culture

This was going to be every bit as difficult a challenge as planting a church, turning a church around, or leading change in a regional setting. This was a national entity with many, many years of tradition and expectations.

The concept of the Director of Missions serving solely as the *"pastor to the pastors"* and the channel of denominational information was deeply embedded in the fabric of the organizations. Although these aspects play a role, they are certainly not the primary focus of the organization.

Donald McGavran wrote a book in the 1950's that dealt with this issue. In the book, *Bridges of God*, he details the early missionary work in areas where the Gospel had not been shared. The missionaries felt a calling from God to go into these very difficult and dangerous places to share the love of Jesus and see the people come to a personal relationship with Him.

Over time the missionaries saw a few people come to Christ but the pace of their missionary endeavor was slow with little tangible results. And then, a disaster happened that caused everyone to focus on ministering to the people in the crisis.

They built hospitals and orphanages to deal with the catastrophe. These are noble and worthy ministries but they were not the primary reason the missionaries had gone to the region. What the missionaries found, however, was a sense of personal value and a larger degree of support from those at home. Slowly over time the hospital and orphanage took more and more of their time and they spent less and less time on reaching the native people. One day the transformation was complete. The primary purpose of being there was now secondary, and the secondary reasons, the hospital and the orphanage, became primary.

The means of measuring the success of their mission shifted from the number of people that were being added to the Kingdom to how the bottom line looked at the hospital and the orphanage.

Another transition occurred with the judicatories that sent the missionaries out with a specific purpose in mind. The judicatories also began to see the hospital and the orphanage as primary, and funding that had originally been allocated to the primary mission was now going to the secondary mission. In reality, the secondary mission had been elevated and accepted as the primary mission and the primary mission of reaching the native people was demoted and accepted as the secondary mission.

The Same Change Occurred in the Association

Associations were formed over 300 years ago with a primary function of helping the churches do together what they could not do alone and provide the churches with a big picture of the missionary impact they could have as they worked together. Over time the Associations became the leaders in the missionary activities the churches felt were part of their vision and calling.

There came a time in the growth of the Southern Baptist Convention that another level of support was needed and the Associations responded by establishing State Conventions. That was a key turning point in the life of the Association. Fairly quickly the State Conventions assumed the role that had been the role of the Association as it related to missionary activity.

The Associations became the point of connection for State Conventions to dispense the information produced by the National Convention. The Associations were the obvious choice since they were the closest entity to the churches. In the context of that day this model worked fairly well and the missionary emphasis saw great gains.

On the flip side, the Associations began to drift away from their primary role as they embraced the role assigned them by the State Conventions. They began to depend more and more on the

State Conventions to respond to the needs of the churches and the Associations began to focus on secondary ministries that over time became their primary ministries.

What Did This Secondary Role Look Like?

The Associations took on the role of the churches as they developed church-type ministries. These ministries included such things as benevolence ministries where the Association would distribute food and clothing on a regular basis. It included Associational evangelism events and camps where the Association would own a camp and host children in the summer.

These are indeed worthy and worthwhile ministries for churches. The Association was not designed to do things that require labor intensive man hours. Churches are designed for the implementation of ministries and follow-up since God gifts and calls church members to serve in certain areas of ministry. For the Association to attempt to carry out these ministries they had to solicit the members of the churches and money from the churches to do the ministries.

Some churches began to see the Association as a competitor for their people's time and resources. Churches in most cases saw themselves as lacking in leaders and funds and when the Association asked the churches to give up a portion of both for the Association to do its ministries they often balked at the request. This was an issue that needed to be resolved.

The Associations had done exactly what McGavran had discussed in his book. They began to see other things as primary, justified why they were doing them, and over time allowed them to become the organization's main priority. I am not assigning blame for anything but simply stating the point in the evolution of Associations at the time I began my work at the North American Mission Board.

The Culture Change Begins

It is one thing to talk about changing a culture but quite another thing to make it happen when you have no authority to do so. Since each Association is autonomous and not subject to any denominational directives it was a much more tedious task to make a system-wide shift.

From my past ministry experience, I knew that the only way to make a lasting difference is to be face to face with as many people as possible to help them understand what a culture change would look like and what it would ultimately mean to their organization. What that meant for me was that by necessity most of my time would be spent outside the office and in the field. This would have a dramatic effect on my personal and family life since in this role the field was all of North America.

When I took the role I did not have any idea that I would spend half my time on the road, but that is exactly what began to happen. The calls for assistance from Associations all across North America grew exponentially, especially after we had developed the Diagnosis and Prescription aspect of our process. No matter how focused the effort was to address all the Associations' needs it was logistically impossible to do so in the desired timeframe.

Even though we were not able to get to every Association right away, the ones we worked with were extremely pleased with what we offered. The change in culture, one Association at a time, was beginning to take effect. Association after Association started to understand the role they had been founded on and how they needed to evolve to play that role again. Once again, churches and their visions were being given encouragement and resources to allow them to do what they could not do alone, and their ministries were not being usurped by another entity. Momentum increased as more and more Associations were able to diagnose the needs of their churches and adopt a prescriptive process to begin to address those needs. All seemed well.

Redefining a Key Role

It was not long before the news of what was taking place in the Associations spread to the state and national levels.

In the early part of my ministry at the North American Mission Board the leadership understood the need for a change and fielded most of the questions related to what I was attempting to do. As long as there was support from the leadership at the Board, the work developed and grew.

A process for determining the Core Competencies for new and potential Directors of Missions was developed. It was determined that one of the key leadership qualities needed in a new Director of Missions was that he needed to be an entrepreneur. There is a great deal of difference between a person presiding over an institution and a person leading. Entrepreneurs look outside their own situation and see a greater picture of how others can play a role in expanding and resourcing their vision.

The new Director of Missions also needed to be a person with a facilitative leadership style. The nature of the work requires a person to be able to clearly share a compelling vision and lead others to own that vision for themselves. Presiders can work alone but good leaders will multiply themselves in others.

The new Director of Missions also needed to be results oriented and not activity oriented. Much of what had been done in the Associations over the last thirty to forty years was activity based. Success was determined by whether the activity was conducted rather than the results that were seen. Much like in McGavran's book, the activity became the primary focus rather than the number of people reached and churches served.

Landscape Changes

The first eighteen months of my time at the Board was challenging and rewarding. There was an opportunity to evaluate the status quo, introduce a new process that was having great results and move quickly toward a tipping point that would change the way Associations functioned.

And then the landscape changed dramatically. The leadership in place when I was called to the North American Mission Board was no longer in place. Every employee in the organization was uncertain what lay ahead and that feeling of uneasiness found its way into the field. Associational leaders were hesitant to commit to changing anything until they knew what was happening to the national leadership and structure of the Board. The transitional period was difficult but no one had any idea what was ahead and how it would affect their lives and ministry.

For me and my family there was uncertainty as well. Pam and I talked often of the place we had left in Phoenix, how much we enjoyed our time there and we even questioned if we had made the right decision to move. It was a time when we had to re-examine the call we believed God had placed on our life. We felt God was active in bringing us to this role and we committed to continue moving forward as long as God allowed us to do so.

Major Changes Happen

After a reasonable transition time new leadership was brought to the Board. It was obvious from the start that the new leadership was very different in style and practice than the leadership I had known. People in various roles at the Board struggled to know the new leadership's vision and how it related to their individual directives. The changes in the amount and qualilty of communication from the leadership began to impact my effectiveness in the field.

I found myself in a crisis moment and one where my faith was once again going to be tested. I did not have any desire to try to usurp the authority of the elected leadership. They were doing what they believed was right and I did not want to try and change their minds. I also did not want to compromise my own beliefs about the vision I was given and the call on my life. So, I was faced with a decision. I could either submit to the authority of the leadership as it was or I could walk away and trust God to open another door.

While I was pondering this decision I was contacted by the California Baptist Foundation about coming to work with them to establish a strong church planting network in California and strengthen the relationship between the Foundation and the local churches. I had declined to entertain this as a possibility at other times when they contacted me, but on this occasion I felt led to at least talk to them.

The Way Becomes Clearer

Feeling unsettled working at the North American Mission Board and increasingly comfortable with the Foundation, Pam and I arrived at a decision. The decision was not an easy one. We could not completely understand why we would be led to Georgia for a period of time and then taken away under these circumstances. At times we felt that we could not trust our decision making process. At this point we were asking the question, why did we leave Phoenix? Through it all we had to look back at what God had done to show us His will.

We had not sought out the North American Mission Board. We were sought out by them. The role we were being asked to do was a great challenge, which was consistent with all of the roles God has called me to. Our house in Phoenix sold before we could ever put it on the market. These were pretty unmistakable indicators of God's involvement, yet the abrupt ending to the time in Georgia made us re-examine it all. In the end we were most concerned about making a decision that would take us away from where God wanted us to be.

Once we made the decision to accept the role at the California Baptist Foundation there was no second guessing and no turning back. God showed Himself clearly in our move to California. He provided a wonderful place for us to live and a challenging vision to achieve. Little did we know we were entering a time that would lead to the greatest test of our faith.

✝ CHAPTER THIRTEEN
One Chapter Closes and a New Chapter Begins

I always believed that as important as it was to begin well in a place of ministry, it was equally important to leave well when the time came. I treated my time at the North American Mission Board with the same respect and desire to end well as I had in other places. This one closed out much more quickly than I thought it might. My ministry positions had been ten years in South Dakota, six plus years in Oklahoma, ten years in Arizona, so to be leaving Georgia after only three years was indeed different. I held out hope that some of what I helped begin there would survive and thrive over the years. As I look back now, that hope became a reality. The things that were initiated are going strong and are making a difference. With mixed emotions we closed out this chapter of our ministry. We were thankful for the opportunity and for the many people we developed friendships with all over the country but we were sad that we did not see the completion and fruition of what we had started.

Once again I found myself in a new field with nothing to use as a reference. I was asked to come to California to give birth to a new ministry that would provide a platform to encourage and facilitate key churches in the state to become involved in church planting and to make a Kingdom difference. That meant determining what it would look like, what it would and would not do, who it would make the focus of its efforts, what protocols would be needed to be successful, and what would be the measure of success. I had built programs and systems from scratch before so I was not over-whelmed by the challenge.

There were other challenges that would make the transition dif-ficult. The economic situation in America had changed dramatically and houses were selling much more slowly than they had a few years earlier. Pam and I decided that I would make my way to California alone with the bare necessities of the work, and once the house in Georgia sold she would follow.

That sounded like a great plan except for the fact that the house was not going to sell. Many would look but no one would make an offer. Finally after several months we decided to make the move to California and continue to try to sell the house.

Finally together after being apart for several months, estab-lishing a new life began in earnest. We rented a home on the east side of Clovis, California on five acres with a clear view of the snow capped mountains in the distance. We were only thirty minutes from the beauty and majesty of Yosemite National Park where the giant Sequoia trees grew. We were surrounded by fruit trees and almond trees and grape arbors. Southern California and the beach were just a few hours away. The Foundation was a well-respected entity that had seen many years of strong ministry and financial success. At first glance this seemed to be the right place for us and we settled in to stay perhaps for the remainder of our ministry.

I spent the first few weeks getting settled and establishing the new ministry and how it would interact with everything else the Foundation offered. Church plants could benefit from the training the Foundation could offer as well as the financial assistance. I visited many of the area churches and pastors as well as the Directors of Missions I had worked with while at the North American Mission Board. The transition to California seemed to go smoothly and without incident.

The Work Gets Underway

As with any new ministry it was important for me to determine if what we were planning to offer was of benefit and would meet the needs that had been identified or if it needed to be altered to be more effective.

I knew the church planting process was one that had worked in many different venues and especially well in the western part of the United States. I wanted to find out what was being done in church planting in the state and determine how to best integrate this new ministry. I spoke with many of the pastors and Directors of Missions in listening forums as I sought a base of knowledge about the health of California churches in general and the nature of church planting in the state.

I found the pastors and other leaders eager to see a process like the one I proposed implemented in the state in order for strong and healthy churches to be started. There were churches being planted but the church planting system that I offered provided a clear roadmap for the church planter to be able to understand his role in moving his new church toward the desired goals.

A New Way of Using the Process

The church planting process was very effective but had also been used to assist existing churches to define their current situation and where they wanted their church to go in the years ahead. The

Foundation had seen a few churches struggle at times to make their loan payments but it was never a big issue. But the economy was changing and churches that had never had an issue paying their loans were experiencing financial difficulty and having problems making payments.

Realizing that the church planting process had the elements in it to assist these churches to become solvent, the Foundation let me work with a couple of the churches to show them what they needed to do to be strong and healthy again.

Thus began an immense undertaking for me. I saw the need to develop and expand my church-planting process to make it universally useful to churches at all levels as a consultation tool. Over the next several months I refined the process and ultimately created the *Count the Cost* process being used today within the *MARKIV CHURCH SOLUTIONS*.

Storm Clouds Form on the Horizon

The economic situation in the United States took an even more serious downturn during my tenure at the California Baptist Foundation. At first no one seemed concerned. There had been downturns before and the Foundation had planned well for them and had significant reserves in place to weather any storm, or so they thought. This downturn was different than any other in the past.

By the end of our first year in California, the situation was becoming severe. The economy had not bounced back and instead continued to fall, creating an increasingly serious situation with the Foundation's financial ability to fund ministries.

The primary income for the Foundation came through the process of granting loans to churches. During this economic crisis, lines of credit were eliminated by the banks. Since those lines of credit were the sources of lending capital for the Foundation, it lost its primary income source.

Once the lending aspect of the Foundation was halted the crisis became even more severe. At the time, the reserves were still covering the shortages and as long as the economy turned around in a reasonable amount of time all would be fine. But the economy did not turn around.

The Double Whammy

When it looked like things could not get worse, they did. Churches were feeling the impact of the economic situation and were falling behind on their loan payments. The Foundation was doing everything it could to help the churches keep their facilities. Loans were renegotiated so payments could be lowered and churches could ease the pressure on their budgets. The problem was that the Foundation's second income stream came from the difference in the amount the Foundation paid for the money and at what rate the churches were able to borrow the money. When the loans were renegotiated the Foundation lost that spread income and added to the internal crisis.

Over the previous years the Foundation saw great growth and expansion requiring more employees. Now there were more employees than there was need for them. With deep sadness the Foundation began to let people go to reduce the cash shortages. Some of these people had worked there many years and never would have thought this day was coming.

I am Affected

Having a solid understanding of how businesses operate and how they deal with the circumstances they face, I knew the Foundation leadership would be assessing possible budget cuts and structure reorganization.

During this time, the churches that had expressed interest in planting new churches had to table those possibilities in order to survive. Since the facilitating of new church plants was my primary role at the Foundation, I knew my position was at risk and found myself in a situation in which I had never been. I knew that if I were the one making these difficult decisions, my position was an obvious one to be eliminated. Anticipating that possibility I began to check out what other ministry and job opportunities might be available to me should this happen.

The landscape was bleak. Everyone had gone into a holding pattern. Turnover in churches had slowed dramatically since houses would not sell and people often owed more on their mortgage than their house was worth. No one was willing to add staff so my options appeared very slim to say the least.

Salaries at the Foundation were cut drastically in an effort to avoid further layoffs, but unless the economy turned upward quickly I knew layoffs were inevitable. Although I knew the possibilities, I did not stop doing what I could to help. I also ramped up the effort to copyright the Church Planting Process before anything might happen. I thought I could fall back on consulting if I needed to provide my own income. Thankfully today the *Count the Cost* process is copyrighted under the *MARKIV CHURCH SOLUTIONS* umbrella, a company that I formed while at the Foundation.

Despite all the valiant efforts of the Foundation, the day came when I was told that I no longer had a position with the company and had six weeks of insurance and salary coverage before it all faded away.

Pam and I had known that this day might come but as I found out, you are never really ready for it when it happens. So many things went through my mind. The first was: what now? I had no options at that point and the holidays were coming up so I knew that any possible church role would not happen for many months.

We did what we have always done and took it to the Lord. We were back in a position where our very sustenance was totally in His hands. He could do with us whatever He desired and we were fine with that outcome. To be in His will and have nothing of the world is truly better than to have many earthly things and not have Him in your life.

Once we had placed it in His hands we set our focus on what needed to happen next. There were a couple of things that as we look back now were blessings we did not see as blessings then. First of all, our house in Georgia had not sold over the two years we were gone. We had not even had an offer even though we had dropped the price over 30% in that timeframe. We asked the Foundation to consider moving us back to our home in Georgia and they graciously agreed.

✝ CHAPTER FOURTEEN
The Dark Days of Transition

Once back in Georgia I began in earnest talking to friends, family, churches and anyone else I could think of to see what God might open up for us, but there was nothing. It seemed we were in the wilderness and even though many people wanted to help us they were not in a position to do so. We found ourselves back where we were thirty years prior, trusting God for everything including health since we could lose our insurance coverage and with preexisting conditions maybe never get it back.

Several places I checked to see what might be available said they would love to have me but there was a hiring freeze and their hands were tied. I knew my calling to be involved in church planting was still valid. I knew God had not withdrawn His hand from my life so I pressed on.

Central Association in Phoenix where I had served as the Director of Missions had a church planter strategist position available, but it required North American Mission Board commissioning to be eligible to serve in that position and receive funding. I talked with the new Director of Missions and he offered to have me come on an open timeline, meaning I could be there as long as I chose to be but if God opened up a new avenue of ministry I would be free to pursue it.

I would be able to start the day my insurance and salary were scheduled to run out in October, but there was one problem. The North American Mission Board would not fund the position until all the interviews and paperwork had been filed and the Trustees voted on it. I knew that process well and knew it would be January before that happened which was well beyond my deadline to keep my health insurance.

When the Association heard that the North American Mission Board would take three months to get me in the system they decided to cover me through the Association and cover all of my insurance. I will be forever grateful for their care and concern for me and my family. The greatest concern was that I would have to leave Pam in Georgia and I would stay with friends in Phoenix until the house was sold and she could come to be with me in Phoenix.

Pam and I determined this was what we were to do at that moment in time so I loaded the bare necessities in my car and drove to Phoenix to begin my service there as a church planter strategist. Pam would work again to try to sell the house and make another transition.

I always enjoyed Phoenix so there was no adjustment needed. I knew all of the people and the churches as well as the area so I was very comfortable from the first day. The people I was working with were good friends whom I loved and respected, so it was a good fit. However, I never felt that this was where I would be long-term. But even though I thought it might be temporary, I continued to do the same kind of work I had always done, and was able to do more for church planting in Arizona and continue to fulfill my vision.

Step By Step

During my time in Phoenix I worked with churches that were planting other churches as well as with existing churches facing difficulties. I found the work I had done to refine the *Count the Cost* process and develop *MARKIV CHURCH SOLUTIONS* was proving valuable. I felt I was an asset to the work in Phoenix and not simply someone they were taking care of in a personal crisis.

I also worked on getting the paperwork done for the North American Mission Board so I could be approved as quickly as possible. We determined if the commissioning happened before the house sold we would move to Phoenix and continue to try to sell the house. When I came back to Atlanta for the interviews it was great to see Pam and be home for a while but it was also awkward. People were interviewing me in some of the same rooms I had interviewed others when I served there. People who were interviewing me knew me well since they were my colleagues not that long ago.

I passed the interviews and waited on the Trustees to meet and vote. Thanksgiving came that year and Pam came out to Phoenix to share that special occasion with our friends and family there. It was a great time but still nothing was on the horizon other than the North American Mission Board appointment. There had been people looking at the house but no offers.

Then it Happened

Just before Christmas I received a call from Pam that a young couple had looked at the house three times and had made an offer. It was our first offer and of course it was well below what it needed to be. We were just hoping to break even with what was owed knowing we would lose all equity we had invested in this house and have no down payment for another house. If we accepted this offer and signed the papers we would be headed to Phoenix with virtually nothing and would be starting over at the age of 56.

We made a counter offer. They made a counter offer. We made a firm counter offer. They made another counter offer. We made our final offer. They accepted it. It was up to us to decide if we were willing to sign the papers and begin a new chapter in Phoenix.

It was at that moment I received a call on my cell phone from Pastor Johnny Hunt. His first question to me was, have you sold your house yet? I said no but we have a negotiated offer on the table. He then said, do not sign any papers. I want to talk with you about coming to serve on staff at First Baptist Church Woodstock.

I asked him what he wanted me to do and he said he wanted me to lead the Church Planting Ministry of the church. As we continued to talk I became convinced that God had shown up once more in His timing and provided the best opportunity to live out my calling and my passion in a church that has a history of church planting. By the time the conversation was over I knew we were going to join the staff at Woodstock.

I talked to Pam and she was excited about it. We told the realtor we had decided not to sell the house and that God had provided a great opportunity in the area. That was not received well by the realtor who had shown the house countless times over two years or by the young couple who thought they had found their dream house. I talked to the Association in Phoenix and they were amazed at what God had done and were very happy for us. I talked to the North American Board and they were shocked that I would not go through the commissioning service as planned.

So, I gave a two week notice at the Association and once that time was done I loaded my things back in my car and drove back home to Atlanta to begin a new and very exciting adventure.

Time to Thank God

Before I begin to share about the current chapter in my life-journey of faith and church planting I want to pause and give thanks to God for what He has done.

God saved me out of circumstances where the odds were not good that anyone would be saved. He placed a call on my life and gifted me to be able to serve Him in ministry. He gave me a beautiful and godly woman to be my wife with whom I have shared this incredible journey. He gave me two amazing children who have grown up to become godly adults. He has given me very interesting and challenging assignments in very unique places. He has at times blessed us with plenty and other times sustained us. He has protected us when we have made choices that were not the best choices to make. He has always been faithful and true to His promises and to His Word. He brought me to the doorway of another assignment that carries with it more responsibility and more possibility than I have known to this point. For these things and many more I am truly humbled and thankful that He would entrust to me such a responsibility.

✝ CHAPTER FIFTEEN
Woodstock:
The Great Adventure Continues

First Baptist Church, Woodstock, Georgia is a church with a wonderful history and heritage dating back many years, but the last twenty-five years under the leadership of Pastor Johnny Hunt have been extraordinarily blessed of God. First Baptist Church Woodstock twenty-five years ago was a downtown church with an attendance of 200-250. Like many churches in our country there had been some internal issues that caused the church to struggle to grow and at times created discord in the fellowship.

After years of struggle the church extended a call to Pastor Johnny Hunt who at the time was thirty-three years old and had been pastoring close to six years. When the church issued the call to Pastor Johnny, he accepted and the beginning of a remarkable relationship was set in motion.

Through the years the church has experienced phenomenal growth and expansion that has not been experienced by many other churches anywhere in the country. The church outgrew the facilities downtown and decided to relocate and build a new facility. Not long after it was completed and the growth continued the church expanded once again and built the current facility on 90 plus acres in Woodstock, Georgia. Today the church will see 6,000-8,000 on any given Sunday with at least 85% – 90% of those attending involved in small group Bible Study on Sunday morning.

Known nationally and internationally as a church that believes in and preaches the Word of God with boldness and clarity, First Baptist Church Woodstock has become one of the most recognizable churches in our time. The church is involved in mission causes and has more than one hundred families on the mission field today that came from First Baptist Church.

Woodstock is also known for something else, namely, its fervor and commitment to seeing new churches started in all parts of the United States and around the world. Over the past twenty-five years the church has been involved in the start of ninety new churches. That is a remarkable record and speaks to the missionary and pioneer spirit of the church and its leadership.

A Great Past Leads To a Great Future

Some churches would be content with what they accomplished in the past but First Baptist Church Woodstock sees an even greater future ahead as the Day of the Lord approaches.

One of the ways the church is preparing for even greater days ahead is by putting an increased emphasis on both its mission endeavors and its church planting process. Over the years the Missions Ministry of the church has been a stand out ministry. It involves many people as they prepare to take the Good News into all parts of the world. Personally, I have never seen a more *going* or a more *giving* church in my 36 years of ministry.

Within the Missions Ministry of the church was a church planting element. Since it was part of the Missions Ministry with many other priorities, it was not seen as the major priority that it could be. The Church Planting Ministry was always funded through *"over and above the tithe"* giving and was never part of the operating budget of the church. For the church to have been involved in ninety church plants with the structure that was in place is a remarkable thing in and of itself.

Renewed Enthusiasm for Church Planting

In the latter part of 2009 when Pastor Johnny Hunt contacted me to ask me to consider coming to First Baptist Church Woodstock to serve as the Minister of Church Planting, he shared that a renewed focus was to be placed on church planting. He wanted to give me the opportunity to develop the church planting structure and processes, and also to design a First Baptist Church Woodstock Church Planting School.

We knew that this was where God wanted us to serve. I also felt a great comfort level in the fact that the *MARKIV CHURCH SOLUTIONS* process was the key piece to assist First Baptist Church Woodstock to have a premier Church Planting Ministry. I will always be thankful for my time in California that allowed me to develop and refine this process. Virtually everything that has since been developed for use at Woodstock has come from *MARKIV CHURCH SOLUTIONS*.

The role I was asked to take seemed to me to be the role God had been preparing me to do for over thirty years. I was not sure about the Church Planting School aspect since I had never done that before, but I believed as always with the call comes the ability to carry out the call. With great excitement and a greater sense of humility, I began my new role with one of the greatest churches of our day.

The Church Planting Ministry was removed from the Missions Ministry and given its own place in the structure and priorities of the church. For the 2011 budget year the Church Planting Ministry was placed into the general operating budget of the church for the first time. That made a major statement as to where church planting stood in the ministry of the church.

My Family and Friends are Excited for Us

It was clear to Pam and I that God was drawing us back to Georgia and putting me into the role that He had been preparing me for all these years. As my friends heard about it they were very excited and to some degree surprised that I was serving at Woodstock. Everyone had heard of the church and saw it as a very high honor to serve there, as do I. I would not have expected this to be my place of service but God in His sovereignty knew before the foundation of the world that I would be here at this time in history for a specific purpose that He had gifted me to fulfill.

People I worked with over the years in virtually every part of our country expressed their excitement for where God had placed me. I saw those relationships as being a great advantage as I assumed this role and continue to seek to establish strong, healthy, reproducing churches in much of the underserved areas of our country.

I see the time at the California Baptist Foundation as vital in allowing me to develop and copyright the *Count the Cost* process for Church Planting under *MARKIV CHURCH SOLUTIONS*. The time I spent in South Dakota helped me understand where the majority of our church plants will find themselves at their beginning. The time in Oklahoma gave me a great perspective of what can divert a church away from church planting and how it can be brought back to a place of reaching out beyond itself. Without a doubt, our time in Phoenix was the laboratory for many of the things learned and practiced dealing with new churches starting in strength not survival. My time serving with the North American Mission Board allowed me the opportunity to meet people, form friendships, and develop a network across the United States and beyond.

✝ PART TWO:
Church Planting: The Nuts and Bolts

✝ CHAPTER SIXTEEN
Getting Started:
MARKIV CHURCH SOLUTIONS

What a tremendous task lay ahead of me as I started this new role. I felt it was important to determine what the Church Planting Ministry for the First Baptist Church of Woodstock should look like and what it would and would not do. With that in mind, I began to develop the process.

The remainder of this book will be used to describe and outline the processes, procedures, and protocols for the Church Planting Ministry to provide the best opportunity for new churches to be planted in such a way to ensure their growth, development and reproduction.

✝ MARKIV CHURCH SOLUTIONS
Church Planting System

✝ CHURCH PLANTING MINISTRY
Purpose

The Purpose of the Church Planting Ministry:

Facilitate the development of strong, healthy, reproducing church plants utilizing the strength and expertise of all partners.

✝ CHURCH PLANTING MINISTRY
Mission

The Mission of the Church Planting Ministry:

Impact the Kingdom of God by serving the underserved through the establishment of strong, healthy, reproducing churches in areas where the evangelical witness is not strong.

† CHURCH PLANTING MINISTRY
Defined

The Church Planting Ministry is defined by:

A belief that there is no substitute for a leader with God's call.

A belief that church planting can have predictable results when certain elements are brought together in sufficient quantity for a sufficient period of time.

A belief that results matter more than activity.

A belief that missions is essential to the success of every church plant.

A belief that everything rises and falls at the point of execution and implementation.

A belief that adaptability and relevance to context are essential.

A belief that accountability must be part of the design and not taken for granted.

A belief that balance is essential to the success of the new church plant.

A belief that discipline must be exercised to achieve the desired outcomes.

A belief that reproduction is natural and not optional.

✝ CHURCH PLANTING MINISTRY
Distinguishing Characteristics

Focus on four crucial areas necessary for the new church to be successful:

- **The Person** (church planter)
- **The Place** (location and context for the new church)
- **The Plan** (Development of a Business and Ministry Plan)
- **The Partnership** (Engaging other Kingdom-Minded entities to partner together)

Focus on all stages of the new church's formation and development.

Focus on clear and pragmatic results-based implementation.

Focus on the importance of balance and discipline within the agreed upon plan.

Focus on incorporating stewardship's best practices to ensure strength.

Focus on intentional reproduction as part of the DNA of the new church.

† CHURCH PLANTING MINISTRY
Non-Negotiables

The church planter must be able to demonstrate God's call on his life for church planting.

The priority of missions must be a key part of the new church plant's ministry.

The place where the new church is being started must be an evangelically underserved area.

The new church plant must have a *Count the Cost* Business and Ministry Plan in place before the new church is launched and demonstrate the discipline to adhere to the plan.

The accountability factor is not an option and must be a high priority programmed into the church planting process.

The partnership support must be present to allow the church to operate within the balance outlined in the Business and Ministry

Plan before the church is launched.

The new church must be birthed with the DNA for reproduction.

✝ CHURCH PLANTING MINISTRY
The Church Planting Process

God places a location on the heart of the church or a potential church planter.

The location is researched to determine context and culture.

Needs are defined to determine the cost of the new church plant from its inception until it is able to operate independently.

Resources and potential partners are identified.

A *Count the Cost* Business Plan is developed and adopted (with the pastor if he is on the scene) that addresses the needs and growth results necessary to meet those needs.

Partnership is formed and agrees to the stipulations in the Partnership Covenant.

The church planting pastor is called by the sponsoring church.

A Ministry Plan is developed with the pastor.

Launch date is set.

New church is launched.

Partnership meetings ensure accountability and support throughout the growth stages of the new church plant.

✝ CHURCH PLANTING MINISTRY
Will Do... Will Not Do

It is our belief that church planting is not a hit and miss game. We believe there can be predictable results if steps are taken in the preparation and development stages that bring the elements of success together. Much like the meteorologist who interrupts the programming on television to make the announcement that severe weather is probable because the elements have come together that create severe weather, it is our belief that if the needed elements are in place, certain results are predictable as they relate to the success of the church plant.

The Person

Without question the first and most critical element in the success of a new church is the Church Planter. Every church planter brings his unique giftedness and personality to the new church but there are certain things that each church planter must also possess.

A Call from God: This may seem obvious but there are many people who have chosen a career path rather than possessing a call from God. The Church Planting Ministry will not partner with someone who cannot clearly articulate their call to be a church planter. It is this call that will sustain the church planter during the challenging and difficult times he and his family will face in their new church. Serving in an area that is underserved by evangelical churches will in and of itself mean that he will have to rely more on his relationship with God than on a network of like-minded people within a close proximity. His call from God means it is not about him, but about reaching people for the Kingdom, discipling them, and deploying them in service.

A Heart for People: As the new church begins there is a great probability that it will not have the best facilities in town or the best equipment in town or even the best ministries in town. What it must have is a person who loves people and has a passion for seeing them come into the Family of God. Having a genuine leader will draw people to a church even when the best of everything is not yet available. The Church Planting Ministry will not work with a church planter with a personal agenda or one that does not love people who do not know Christ. People need to know that they are loved by this man of God, and if they know that they often will be willing to overlook issues that arise in a new church.

A Teachable Spirit: If a person believes they have all the answers and are not willing to learn from others they will likely fail. The Church Planting Ministry cannot help a person with all the answers, who stands in need of nothing. To understand that each of us have weaknesses and acknowledge those weaknesses is the first step to finding a way to work through them. There is an important difference between listening to your critics and listening to your mentors. Without a teachable spirit, you may not know the difference.

Visionary: The new church planter must be able to clarify in his mind what the new church will be and do and provide a preferred future for those who are reached. He must have the ability to articulate this vision in such a way that the people in the church understand it and can help fulfill it. The Church Planting Ministry can assist the pastor in casting this vision.

Doctrinal Alignment: Every person has the right to determine their own belief system. Each church must determine what it will and will not accept. The Church Planting Ministry recognizes that the partnership we will have with a church planter requires a greater level of commonality and trust than other relationships. The following serve as examples of what the Church Planting Ministry considers important areas of alignment between sponsor church and church planter.

Missiology – a church planter supported by the Church Planting Ministry must share the view of the Church Planting Ministry regarding God's mission and how the church should respond to Acts 1:8. He will make it a priority from the onset as evidenced in how he leads his new congregation towards their personal involvement

Ecclesiology – a church plant sponsored by the Church Planting Ministry must share its view regarding the nature and purpose of the local church. The new church plant sponsored and supported by the Church Planting Ministry will work in partnership with the Church Planting Ministry and will not exercise unilateral autonomy. As a supporter, the Church Planting Ministry retains the right to have a voice and influence in the decision-making of the new church plant.

Purity and Holiness – the ends never justify the means! No goal is important enough to sacrifice biblical truth to achieve. The Church Planting Ministry will not support or condone any action of the church planter that would violate the morals and the ethics laid out in the Word of God.

High Standard of Personal Qualities: In a partnership based on trust and accountability it is essential that all parties agree on the standards of conduct laid out in God's Word.

Following are some of the characteristics the Church Planting Ministry believes are most important for a church planter with whom we can partner:

Called of God

Heart for People

Humble/Teachable/Tenacious Commitment

Team Player/High Personal Integrity/Inspiring Leader

Pure/Passionate/Authentic/Focused/Responsible/Articulate/Adaptable

The Partnership

With the church planter being the most critical of the elements needed for successful church planting, the next ingredient is a close second. The second ingredient is a strong Partnership.

In the world we live in today it is extremely difficult to launch out and start a new church alone. It can be done, but the odds of success are diminished greatly. The best methodology today is to bring together like-minded partners and allow them to add strength and stability to the new church while it is in the developmental stages. Birthing a new church is much like birthing a new baby and giving it warmth, love, nurture, and care until it grows up and is able to take care of itself. Even then, the parent should be available in case of a crisis.

A partnership brings several very important things to the new church:

Clearly Defined Expectations: Issues can arise that may hinder a new church if things are being done months after the church began that were not in the original discussions of the partners. A partnership can clearly define the role and expectations of all partners and develop covenants that specifically spell out the expectations. The Church Planting Ministry will require covenants with the church planter and all partners before any funding will be allocated. Each party will understand and sign the covenant at the beginning of the partnership. In this way the work can move swiftly and without the distraction of unfulfilled expectations.

Accountability: One of the most important roles the partnership will play is that of providing accountability. Once the new church has laid out its growth and development goals the partnership has the responsibility to meet with the church planter regularly. Together, they will determine how the work is progressing, what problems the church planter is encountering, and how the partners might be able to assist the church planter to achieve the agreed upon outcomes. Without accountability as part of the church planting process the odds of success are greatly diminished. The Church Planting Ministry will require a regular and ongoing accountability meeting with the new church planter and any partners to gauge the progress of the new church plant.

Involvement of Other Churches: Each partner church will provide the new church with prayer support, resources, and in many cases manpower to allow the new church to do things that it may not have the ability to do on its own. The Church Planting Ministry will commit to pray faithfully and fervently for the new church and provide as much manpower as distance and context allow.

Within every partnering church are people with extraordinary gifts, talents, and resources that can be utilized to assist the new church. The partnership gives them an avenue and a responsibility to do so.

The Plan

The next key ingredient for successful church plants is The Plan. Many churches are started with a specific idea for a beginning and a vague idea of where the church might end up, but there is little in the middle to serve as a roadmap to get between the two points. If a person decided to take his family on a trip from Los Angeles to New York but had never been to New York, there are certain questions they would ask. Possibly he would want to know the direction to take. To start haphazardly might mean a drive into the ocean which does not achieve his goal of New York. He might want to know the cost of the trip. What are some mile markers along the way to gauge progress? How will he know when he is getting close? People will take hours to plan a road trip and ask many questions but often in church planting the questions are never asked and the plan is never made. The Church Planting Ministry will require each new church plant to have a *Count the Cost* Business Plan and a Ministry Plan in place before they undertake the journey of planting the church. The business plan will take into account the financial needs as well as the growth needed in order to fulfill the agreed upon outcomes. Based on the plan, the partnership will have clearly defined and realistic goals that the new church is attempting to reach, as well as the ministries the new church plans to use to reach the people necessary to grow and reproduce.

The plan will indicate:

- The number of potential attendees the church must have a relationship with in order to achieve their attendance and baptism goals. This will facilitate the development of an outreach plan to identify potential attendees, engage them, reach them, disciple them, and deploy them in service.

- The number of new small groups needed and when. It will also indicate the number of leaders needed and when. By utilizing this plan the new church can know ahead of the need what leaders and small groups will be needed. This will facilitate the development of a leadership development plan so the church is always ready with leaders to equip and disciple those who are reached.

- The amount of resources needed for the church to remain strong and balanced financially. The plan will indicate the per capita giving of each attendee weekly and will give the church the amount of undesignated receipts it can use in the new church. This will facilitate the development of a stewardship plan that will teach church members and potential church members about stewardship and other aspects such as budgeting, investing, etc.

- The amount of partnership needed until the new church is self-sustaining. The Business Plan will indicate what the new church is able to do financially for itself and the difference in what it provides and what is necessary to be successful. That discrepancy represents the amount of funding and the length of partnership needed and for how long. This will facilitate the development of a partnership plan that indicates to potential partners what the church plans to do from the start until it is self-sufficient.

I have found that potential partners are more willing to agree to a partnership when they have a clear idea of what their resources will mean to the new church, how long they will need to provide those resources, and what their exit strategy will be.

The Church Planting Ministry will provide expertise in developing the Business Plan and working with the new church planter to develop the Ministry Plan before the church is launched (See Appendix One).

The Place

Another key element of successful church planting is that of selecting The Place. The location where a new church begins has so many variables that it would be impossible to detail all of them. Sometimes it is where the church planter grew up or where there is a geographical draw. Although in many cases these are viable it is the desire of the Church Planting Ministry to focus on areas that are underserved by the evangelical community.

Every location is possible but that does not mean every location is ideal. We choose to follow these priority protocols in selecting the right places to apply our partnership:

Is this an area that fits within the sponsoring church's mission strategy?

Is this an area underserved by the evangelical community?

Is it a location where the sponsoring church already has partnerships or locations where people groups reside that are already within its mission strategy?

Is it a location where we have experience, understand the culture, and have researched the demographics?

Is it an area that is suitable for a partnership by the sponsoring church's Church Planting Ministry?

Is it an area where we already have existing partnership possibilities?

Is it a place where the context and culture are a good match to the church planter?

† Designing the Church Planting School

Once these foundational pieces were developed and agreed upon by the leadership of First Baptist Church Woodstock, it was time to begin to address the *MARKIV CHURCH SOLUTIONS* Church Planting School sessions. I believe that the sessions should help a church planter, potential church planter, coach, and potential supporting church understand the journey from the start to the time the church is self-sustaining and able to reproduce.

✝ Level 100:

Strength or Survival?

The first class in the series deals with the issues that prevent churches from starting in a strength position. The first critical issue to deal with is the call of the church planter. To be able to stay for the long haul, the church planter must be certain of his call from God to plant a church and have a *whatever it takes* mentality.

Church Planting cannot be based on a career path choice, but rather on a clear and compelling call from God. Serving alone, often-times in an area where evangelical witness is not strong will require the church planter to rely on God more than any other relationship he has at the time.

God's Call Will Produce Several Things in the Church Planter:

First of all, it will produce a heart for people. The new church will likely not have the best of facilities, the best of equipment, or even the best of ministries, but what it needs the most is a person with a clear mandate from God who loves people and has a heart for them to come into the family of God.

Secondly, God's call will produce a genuineness and authenticity that the people are longing to see and that will carry the day when the best of everything is not available.

Thirdly, a call from God will produce a humble and teachable spirit in the church planter. Having a clear call from God lets the church planter know that he is unable to carry out such a tremendous responsibility without God and others joining him. It is not a one man operation. Each church planter must come to a place where he realizes he does not have all the answers and must learn from others or in all likelihood his ministry will not survive. Arrogance has no place in the church planter's life and ministry.

Finally, a call from God produces a life of holiness and purity. The church planter must exemplify at all times the morals and ethics laid out in God's Word. This is not the place to try shock value techniques. The ends never justify the means. No goal or activity is important enough to sacrifice Biblical truth.

God's Call Will Also Require of the Church Planter:

Knowledge of his leadership style and how that can be utilized with potential staff and church members as God gives them to the church.

Honest examination of his doctrinal alignment including his belief structure, ecclesiology, and missiology.

Comprehensive assessment of his personal giftedness and skill set. The assessment is not so much designed to determine if the person can actually be a church planter but more to help us see the areas where we can provide additional support or training to make his opportunity the best one possible.

An evaluation of his strategic capabilities in the areas of vision, entrepreneurship, leadership, execution, and implementation.

The development of a Business and Ministry Plan that will indicate what the preferred future looks like and the means and path necessary to get there.

Identifying, engaging, and enlisting partners to secure their commitment to the vision and desired outcomes, ensuring a greater possibility of the outcomes becoming reality.

What is produced as a result of God's call is in God's hands. Through the work of His Holy Spirit those things will begin to mold the church planter into a workable vessel.

Location, Location, Location

The second element of the *MARKIV CHURCH SOLUTIONS* Church Planting School after a person can clearly articulate their calling, is to take a serious look at the areas where new churches need to be started the most. These areas are what we call the *"underserved"* areas and are made up of sections of the country where the evangelical witness is very small, with generally 10% or less of the overall population classifying themselves as evangelical Christians.

These areas are not where the low hanging fruit is to be found. These are difficult areas of hard ground where the church planter will need every aspect of his call to be able to withstand all the issues he will face.

Know What You Are Getting Into

The third aspect of the *MARKIV CHURCH SOLUTIONS* Church Planting School involves the development of a *Count the Cost* Business and Ministry Plan for the new church based solely on information from its unique context and culture. The process is laid out in the Appendix section of the book, but I want to take a moment to help the reader understand why this process could make a huge difference in how churches are planted today and in the next generation.

Church planting has been a guessing game for years but does not need to be any longer. The *Count the Cost* process based on Luke 14:28 gives the church planter a sense of predictability, clear and attainable expectations, leadership and stewardship development and the ability to see what the future looks like so preparations can be made with confidence. But it does even more than that. It gives the church planter the ability to execute well and against the right things. A church planter only has so much time, money, and manpower so everything that is done must be done with optimum efficiency.

The *MARKIV CHURCH SOLUTIONS Count the Cost* process allows the church planter to execute at optimum efficiency and achieve the best results possible.

By having a clear vision of the future, the church planter can know what needs to be done and when so he is never caught off guard. Simply stated, a vision is a view of the future as we would like for it to be.

Three Main Goals

To establish a healthy, new church there are basically three things that need to happen:

The new church must reach people. If the new church does not reach people who are not Christ followers with the Gospel on a regular and intentional basis the new church will simply not survive. To fail to make the development of an outreach plan a priority is to limit what the new church will be able to do. Unless people are systematically reached for Christ nothing else matters.

The new church must disciple people. Unless those who are reached are taught biblical principles, they will not grow and develop into followers of Jesus. What good is a church whose members remain baby Christians forever, never developing their faith?

The new church must deploy people. There must be clearly defined ways people can serve as well as the freedom to paint outside the lines.

Reaching, discipling, and deploying people are necessary to establishing a new church whether it is located in Alabama or Argentina. What that looks and sounds like and how it is to be accomplished is largely dependent on the pastor of the new church being able to cast a clear and compelling vision.

Creating Your Plan

In the book, *Flawless Execution*, James D. Murphy states that if fighter pilots make a mistake, they die. If something happens they had not prepared for, they die. The stakes are extremely high. As a church planter it is important to understand that you are dealing with high stakes as well. There are eternal consequences for the people in your church and in your community. The stakes could not be higher.

The author goes on to mention that there are no flawless missions. They might appear to us to be flawless but in reality every mission has many things that happen that the pilots had to anticipate and have an answer for in a split second. Every mission is flown by an individual, but each individual is completely dependent on the team for their survival. It all comes down to execution. Individual execution is important but team execution is a must. It is not enough for the church planter to be effective individually, he must also be effective in developing a team that can execute the vision of the future well.

To execute at a high level of success you must begin with a clear picture of the future. In church life we call that vision. It is a well-defined, high resolution, easily communicated picture of what you want the future to be.

In *Flawless Execution* there is this example: Imagine yourself at a baseball game with your friend. You tell him you are willing to buy the hot dogs if he will go to the concession stand and pick them up. Your friend agrees and proceeds to the concession stand with a desire to execute the order to the best of his ability. When he gets to the concession stand does he have a clear enough picture of what your vision of an awesome hot dog really is?

Is your vision of an awesome hot dog one on a plate or one wrapped in paper?

Does it have relish on it?

Is it grilled or boiled?

Do you prefer mustard, ketchup, onions, or green peppers?

Do you prefer it with chili or no chili?

Is your vision of the awesome hotdog the big half pounder or the slim hot dogs you remember as a kid?

Clearly, what you have in mind is pickles, ketchup, onions, on a plate, two napkins, and it had better be the half pounder! In order for your friend to get the order right, did you paint for him a high enough resolution picture to allow him to make your vision a reality? If he is without a clearly defined outcome he will probably bring back something different than what you expected.

The richness and completeness of the picture of the future is what makes it executable. It becomes the beacon in the night. It is what draws people together and gives them the drive and incentive to move forward. It is what provides guidance for all in the church. Every person needs to know and understand the vision and be serious about carrying it out. The people must see what you see or they cannot follow.

Execution is important but execution alone is not enough. You must execute against the right things to be successful. You can execute better than anyone else but if you are executing against the wrong things you will lose.

Church planters are by their very nature entrepreneurs in some form or fashion. Entrepreneurs are the masters of the art of painting a clear picture of the future. Church planters use their high resolution vision of the future in convincing others to invest in their church's future. Partners are more likely to partner with someone casting a clear vision, and will be able to see the benefit of future involvement.

Having a clear vision of the future gives needed direction, but it also can prevent your church from being distracted when other ministry opportunities arise. If something does not contribute to achieving the vision it does not belong on the table. It might be a good thing but it has no place in the process. When creative people understand the desired outcome they are then able to contribute their skill and expertise to fulfill the vision without being sidetracked.

There are basically four questions to think about as you determine your preferred picture of the future and how you believe God would have you carry it out:

Where are we going to be in the future?

What are we going to apply our resources to in order to get there?

How are we going to get there? What is the plan?

When are we going to exit and finish well?

Setup For Success

To be successful and see your new church make a Kingdom difference will take more than just you. You must be able to transfer your vision and passion in high resolution detail to others. You must be able to execute your plan, and the more specific your plan is, the better you will know when you have accomplished it.

The heart of executing your vision is found in three things:

- People

- Strategy

- Operations

Only you as the leader can facilitate the execution of your plan by utilizing these three things. You must carefully choose others for leadership roles. That is a make or break issue in the life of a young church. When the church plant is very small it is also very fragile. For you to place someone in leadership that does not know, understand, and passionately accept the vision of the future is to set yourself up for failure. You must decide who is on the bus and what seats they will occupy. You also must set the strategic direction the church will take to achieve the vision. Whether you want to or not you must deal with operational issues. To say that you are there to preach only is to not understand church planting at all. When you plant a church you are the one responsible for all aspects of the work. Operations are not glamorous but they are necessary. You cannot afford to simply preside over the church, you must lead it.

You as the leader must establish a climate where excellence is expected and execution is done at a high level of success. You are the key ingredient to influence the direction and spirit of your new church. You are the one who must impart the vision to your people but to do that effectively you must know them well. You must always be real and insist that everything you do is based in reality. Realistic expectations are crucial in church planting. You must set clear, high resolution mile markers for your journey that everyone can see and understand. You must always follow through on everything you say and commit to doing. You must design ways to reward those who are getting the job done with excellence. You must know yourself well enough to recognize your weaknesses and bring others around you to compliment your giftedness.

The process also allows a person (possibly from the partnership) to be a coach who will encourage you as well as track important, tangible aspects of the church plant to keep the church moving forward toward its goals.

✝ Level 200:
Issues That Can Sink Your Ship

The 100 Level Church Planting School session, *"Strength or Survival"* deals with the call and passion of the church planter, the areas where churches are needed the most, the design and development of a culturally and contextually based *Count the Cost* Business and Ministry Plan, and identifying, engaging, and utilizing partners to achieve the desired outcomes the new church has established.

Where the Level 100 Course is designed to help the new church planter get started well after first counting the cost, the Level 200 Course: *"Issues that Can Sink Your Ship"* is designed to help the church planter deal with issues along the journey once he has started. Just as the fighter pilots had a briefing before every mission and dealt with every conceivable issue, the church planter must deal with *"Issues That Can Sink Your Ship."* Every church planter will face things he did not expect, but if he has thought through some of the potential issues and developed a plan of action for when they arise, he will have a greater opportunity to successfully deal with the surprises of church planting and complete his journey.

It is the desire of *MARKIV CHURCH SOLUTIONS* to assist in bringing some of these issues to the surface so they can be dealt with in a manner that will not allow them to hinder the growth and development of the new church. Some of the issues that are covered in the 200 Level Course are:

Insecure Leadership: This topic is covered in the first two sessions of the Level 200 Course. This one topic can have the most serious consequences and can actually destroy the new church as well as the family and ministry of the church planter.

Failure to Trust: This topic deals with the church planter and his ability to develop the needed infrastructure for the church to grow and develop in a healthy way. The church planter must learn to trust those around him through equipping them and allowing them to minister or he will not see the new church progress. He must be willing to give the authority as well as assign responsibility to his people. Participants will learn what it takes to give their ministry away and develop comprehensive systems that will ensure the people who are reached will also be discipled and deployed. Participants will be able to begin to identify protocols to help them develop the necessary outreach ministries, leadership development processes, and partnership to strengthen the new church.

Family and Finances: This session addresses the pressures and strains put on families in church plants and how a good financial system is needed both personally and corporately to reduce the pressure on the family. This session utilizes church planters in the field currently dealing with the pressures and how they are coping with them. Participants who have completed the Level 100 Course where the Business and Ministry Plan was introduced will have an opportunity to update and better understand this process.

Facing Fatal Legal Issues Before They Happen: Each new church faces legal issues from the basics of how to get started with taking the first legal offering, submitting Articles of Incorporation, to background checks and any number of potentially fatal issues. To fail to address these potential situations can become a fatal matter for a church at a time they may be doing well. Participants will be able to understand these issues and develop policies and procedures that may save the life of the new church one day.

Following Through with the Implementation of the Vision: The last session in the Level 200 Course will assist the new church planter to aggressively follow through on the original vision. This aspect of the Level 200 Course will challenge the church planter to evaluate what he has been doing as

well as filter everything through the prism of the original vision.

✝ Level 300:
The Kingdom-Minded Church

The Level 300 session continues the journey of the church planter and his church to the point of having a global scope and the ability to reproduce effectively and often.

The topics covered in the Level 300 course begin with the study of what it means to minister as a Kingdom-Minded Leader. You are the leader of your church in vision and perspective. You must possess a heart for reaching people in your community for Christ throughout your church planting process, but also you must be able to keep a broad view of the impact your ministry can make on the world.

Also covered is the development of a Kingdom Mindset. There is the need to establish the reason why something needs to be done before systems and structures can be effectively changed. You must ignite a passion among your church members to reach the world with the Good News. To continually awaken that passion in your church will require more than a passing mention of missions. This session will also help the Kingdom-Minded Leader find his church's best fit for ministering effectively in a global setting.

Finally, the Level 300 course will examine the topic of Multiplication. It needs to be in the fabric of their DNA for churches to reproduce strongly and often. The nuts and bolts of the when, where, how, how much, and by whom the reproducing should occur will be discussed and examined.

✝ CONCLUSION

Church Planting is a dynamic and ever-changing process that cannot be wrapped up in a manual. This book is not a manual but it does introduce you, the church planter and Kingdom-Minded Leader, to a process that is truly owned by you and utilizes your input.

I tell you this story because it is *my* story. A story about a church planter who has been extremely blessed of God. I have made many mistakes but I feel I have learned from each one and became stronger and more capable after each one.

Out of all my experiences God has honed a process that will help church planters and pastors not just survive but thrive in their calling from God. For that I am eternally grateful.

Together, my family and I have helped facilitate the birth of many churches. I hope and pray that through this book and *MARKIV CHURCH SOLUTIONS*, we can help many of you who are doing the same. I know that it is not an easy path to take, and I am praying for every person who reads this book to be blessed by the process and by my story.

To God be the Glory, great things He has done.

✝ APPENDIX ONE
Business and Ministry Plan
Counting the Cost: Luke 14:28

Church plants have difficulty preparing for the future because they do not know what it will look like. There is no lack of assessment tools that will help a pastor understand his leadership style, temperament, and skill set. There is no lack of groups that will share various ways to *"start"* and build a crowd. The piece that seems to be missing is the ability of the new church to see what is ahead and create a timetable based on mile markers along the way. There is usually a starting point and a place the church would like to eventually reach but in most of the information I receive from church planters there is nothing dealing with what the trip looks like and what it takes to get there.

The exercise of taking a road trip with your family from Los Angeles to New York was designed to help each person think through a simple process and ask the appropriate questions to help each of us make the journey safely and successfully. When it comes to planting a church the same principles apply. Questions are raised that deal with the direction you will go, how long it will take, how much it will cost, mile markers to gauge progress, and at what point the journey is accomplished. Without the answers to these questions and appropriate responses to deal with them, the direction may be off, the urgency to move ahead may be lost, the resources needed may be stretched too far, and the ultimate destination may not be achieved.

Oftentimes, new churches are affected by an unforeseen event in the second or third year that proves to be terminal. Had the new church been able to see the devastating event coming from the beginning they could have made provision to deal with it, or even avoided it altogether. On other occasions, decisions and choices are made early in the life of the church without regard for the implications those decisions might have down the road. When asked later if the church would have made the same early decisions after seeing the implications, the answer is often no.

The MARKIV CHURCH SOLUTIONS Count the Cost process will allow each of you to be able to design and utilize a Business and Ministry Plan that is completely based on your context and culture using your input. You will be able to see where you are in your journey and what it will take for you to move to where you want the church to be in a few years.

The Count the Cost Business Plan aspect will show you the broad picture and the road you will travel. It gives insight into the interaction of all the aspects of raising up a new church. For example, the outreach process will lead to new believers coming into the fellowship. There must be adequate space and leadership to begin the discipleship process for the new believers. The Count the Cost process will indicate how many small groups, how many leaders, and what amount of space you will need, based on the people you reach. No longer will the church be caught by surprise and have to scramble to find space or leaders. The new church will be able to be proactive in providing what is needed before it is an urgent need.

The Ministry Plan aspect is the part the pastor and local people must provide. They must pray and strategize the best methodologies in their context to identify, engage, reach, disciple, and deploy the people they reach. They must determine the best activities and events to accomplish their desired outcomes. They must give constant attention to the *Count the Cost* Business Plan in order to know the best time to prepare for the new believers generated from the outreach ministries. The *Count the Cost* Business Plan is the highway to travel on your journey while the Ministry Plan is the fuel for the journey to move you down the highway.

The *MARKIV CHURCH SOLUTIONS Count the Cost* process is based on the belief that there are four key elements needed for a church to be planted in strength, not in survival.

First of all, there is the person of the church planter. To have the wrong person leading the church planting process is to doom it from the start. The single most critical element in the ability of the new church to either flourish or flounder is the person. As we have already heard, the call and passion of the pastor is critical in this process.

Secondly, the place where the church is to be planted is also a key ingredient. What are the characteristics and values of the area? Is the pastor of the new church compatible with the area? What ministries would best address the expressed needs in the community? How could the ministries be used to bridge into a communication of the Gospel?

Thirdly, the plan is a crucial ingredient in the success of the new church. This does not refer to an overarching, broad brush approach. The plan would be a fairly detailed glimpse into the future showing the various growth and development stages the new church will pass through and what must be done to make the journey effectively. This is, in my opinion, the ingredient that is missing most often as I talk to church planters. They have the broad brush grand scheme of things in their mind but it is the details that will drive it along. Without the mechanisms in place to move towards the vision, it is simply a dream with no substance. The *Count the Cost* process addresses this ingredient in a very clear way.

The fourth key ingredient is partnership. Today, very few churches have the ability to launch churches with the strength they need without the help of other partners. The issue becomes for the potential partners, how much, for how long, and what is the desired outcome? Without a *Count the Cost* process it is a guessing game at best. For each of us to be good stewards we must have a more predictable process that shows us the amount and type of support needed, and how long the commitment would last. The issue for the new church is clarifying what they want to achieve and then establishing the process to get there.

I am often asked how there can be any predictability in planting a church. I answer them with this story: I grew up in Oklahoma in the middle of *"Tornado Alley."* Every spring the potential for severe storms is higher than any other time of the year. In fact, the weather man would interrupt my favorite program fairly often to announce that the conditions were favorable for severe storms to develop in these counties, and he would list the counties and draw a box around them. With uncanny accuracy severe storms would develop in those counties. I wondered why not the whole state? Why just these counties? How did he know that?

I later found out that when certain elements in the atmosphere are brought together and allowed to interact that there would be predictable results. That is how he knew where these storms would develop. The elements needed were all present and interacting.

The same is true of church planting. When the elements we listed earlier are present there can be a much greater predictability for results than if they are not there. What the *Count the Cost* process will do is indicate for you what the predictable results are based on the information you provide from your ministry field. Keep in mind that this is not a Georgia thing or a Woodstock thing but is uniquely yours and it will only give a glimpse into the future for your situation.

Look at the spreadsheet first. You can download a copy of this file at markivchurchsolutions.com. Under church planting click on the *Count the Cost* file. The formulas are included in the file but are password protected since this process is copyrighted under the *MARKIV CHURCH SOLUTIONS* banner. There are four sections to this file. For assistance in using the spreadsheet process and follow along using a sample church file, contact Bill Agee at **markivchurchsolutions.com**.

First is the Data page. This is the page where your individual and unique data is entered to begin the *Count the Cost* process. In the shaded cells you will find the Church Name, City, State, Date the *Count the Cost* process is completed, and the current compensation for all staff including benefits if any.

In the shaded cells in the middle of the page are places to enter acreage, price per acre, square footage of the facility, cost per square foot, cash on hand, indebtedness, and the amount of any loan and the interest rate, all of which will indicate the cost for facilities.

In the shaded cells at the bottom of the page you will find the per capita giving, which is the amount each attendee brings to the offering plate each week on average. In these shaded cells you will also find the percentage of growth the new church must achieve to reach the agreed upon goals and the amount of rent or debt retirement each month.

Next to the shaded areas is the average attendance required to stay on track as you move along in your journey. Next to that you will find the amount of undesignated giving which comprises the new church's portion of the budget.

The second section of the file is the actual *MARKIV CHURCH SOLUTIONS Count the Cost* spreadsheet. This page recounts and shows what is needed to achieve the goals based on the input from the data page. Line 2 gives us the current year and continues for five years. Line 3 is the beginning of the Assumptions section. There are assumptions made because in most cases the new church does not have any concrete information to share. Everything is speculative at this point.

Lines 7-9 are very important lines. These lines indicate the number of starting relationships and relationship goals needed to achieve the desired attendance. By relationship I am referring to someone in the new congregation that knows someone who is not a regular attendee of any church and could possibly attend the new congregation if asked by the person with the relationship. The assumption made for the Sample Church was a starting attendance of 25. In order to have 25 as an average attendance the new congregation must identify and engage 42 potential attendees. To grow to an average of 42 the church need to have relationships with 94 potential attendees. The question becomes what the new church will do to identify and engage 52 new potential attendees to see 31 of them become attendees of the church.

This is where the new church would benefit from a clearly defined outreach plan that would put them on a direct collision course with people in their community. (A worksheet with key questions is included in the appendix section of this book.) If there is not a workable outreach plan developed, the other things we will talk about are irrelevant. If the new church simply focuses on activities and not results, it will not survive. The new church must reach people for Christ before seeing any growth or reproduction.

In the underserved areas there will not be many that will transfer a church letter and join from another church. The new congregation needs a focused and intentional outreach plan to accomplish their desired outcome.

Once the new church begins to reach people they must be able to provide adequate leadership and opportunity for the new believers to begin being discipled. The *Count the Cost* process will indicate for the pastor and his leadership team how many and when small groups will be needed, as well as how many new leaders must be trained in order to be ready when the growth occurs. Waiting until the growth happens will be too late. The pastor must be able to anticipate and the *Count the Cost* process allows him to be more proactive than reactive.

Line 20 indicates the number of people that can be expected to attend at 80% capacity and 100% capacity of the facility. This is critically important to understand because in the sample church process the new church will reach an attendance of 113 (Line 9) by the end of the second year. The capacity at 80% is 91 people. The new church will need to be prepared for multiple services by the end of the second year. When should the preparation begin to be ready by the end of the second year? Certainly not at the end of the second year. The *Count the Cost* process allows the pastor and his leadership to see when the facility will impede their growth and they will know months in advance to prepare for the additional people.

Lines 30-34 indicate the fiscal balance needed for the church to grow at an optimum rate. Over the years the best ratios have proven to be not more than 40% of the undesignated income of the new congregation be used for personnel costs, and 30% be allocated to cover facilities. This is an important number because if the church does not set this aside early in its life, when the cost of a new facility arises the new church will have a very difficult time finding the extra amount needed to pay for the new facility. 20% is available for ministry and 10% for missions, to be broken down as the new church sees fit. If there are state and Associational partners involved, those numbers may change slightly. Once the new church can determine what it has available to use for personnel, facilities, ministry, and missions it is easily determined how much is needed in each area to be solvent.

Line 40 indicates the amount the new church can use for personnel costs. In this case the amount is 40% of the budget divided by 12 for a total of $1,453 per month. According to line 11 the amount needed for personnel is $60,000 or $5,000 per month. What that means is there is a need for $3,547 per month from additional partners to cover the cost of personnel. As the church grows and the 40% allocated for personnel increases the amount needed from partnership decreases accordingly.

Line 49 indicates the 20% amount available for ministry. Oftentimes people will say that this is not very much but it is more than you think since you only have 25 people at this point.

Line 58 indicates the 30% available for facilities is $1,090. According to line 16 the rent cost is $2,500 leaving $1,410 to be covered by partnership.

The bottom line is found in lines 74 and 76. In year one the amount needed by the new church to operate at the agreed upon starting points is $59,479. $42,560 is personnel and $16,919 is facility costs. In year two the amount needed drops to $41,374. $26,428 is personnel and $14,946 is facility costs. In year three the new church is able to operate without outside partnership and shows a significant surplus in personnel and facility costs in years four and five. The new church could afford more space and safely add staff in those years. The total amount needed for this church to grow from 25 to 400 in five years is $100,853. There is no longer a guessing game regarding how much support is needed or for how long.

The third page is the Financials page and shows the undesignated giving of the church as it would be allocated in the four key areas. If the funds are allocated as the Business Plan indicates the church will not find itself out of balance or in financial disarray.

The fourth page is the Computations page. This displays the growth pattern over the next five years, month by month. A pastor and his leaders can look at this and not be blindsided by anything in the future. For those of you serving as church planter network leaders or as coaches for church planters, this is a key piece of your arsenal. You now have month by month tangible outcomes to coach to in every category. This piece has been the *"aha"* moment for many church planters and church planting facilitators.

Now turn your attention to the accompanying document. This contains a recap of the current data, the assumptions made and agreed upon by all parties, observations, and critical issues to consider. The critical issues deal with the Outreach Plan and what the elements of an outreach plan are. A worksheet is included in Appendix Two of this book to assist a church planter and his people to develop and critique their outreach plan. If this piece does not work, everything else is irrelevant. A second critical issue is the Leadership Development Plan. Once the new church can see from the *Count the Cost* process what the growth will look like they will be able to determine how many leaders they will need, but the critical element of this plan is what the leaders need to know and be taught. There is another worksheet in the notebook that will assist a church planter and his people to develop and critique their leadership development plan. A third critical issue is the Stewardship Plan. The new church must demonstrate, teach and instill biblical stewardship in the people they reach. A worksheet is included in the notebook to assist a church planter and his people to develop and critique their stewardship plan. A fourth critical issue is the Partnership Plan. The new church will need to secure additional partners to carry out its vision. A worksheet is included in the notebook that will assist a church planter and his people to develop and critique their partnership plan. Securing partners will be much more effective if the new church utilizes the *Count the Cost* process as they share with potential partners. A potential partner wants to know how much is needed, for how long, and what the outcome will be. This process allows a church planter to clearly show a partner what is needed, for how long and even in what area.

✝ APPENDIX TWO
Development of the Ministry Plan

OUTREACH MINISTRY PLAN

Briefly review the Business Plan:

Clarify issues

Answer questions

Determine level of church commitment to and buy-in for the Business Plan

Address the key issues identified in the Business Plan

Outreach Ministry Plan: This issue addresses the plan and process the church will utilize to identify and engage potential attendees, train church members in outreach strategies and methodologies, and provide follow-up for those accepting Jesus Christ as their Savior so they can get connected and begin their journey in the faith.

Goal number of potential attendees to reach according to the Business Plan _____.

Evaluation of the current outreach ministry plan:

What is being done?

Is it random happenings or part of a unified plan?

Are there clearly defined outcomes?

Is there adequate training for those implementing the project?

Is there a well defined follow-up plan?

What, in your opinion, could improve the current outreach plan?

Discuss elements of a potential outreach plan

What activities would be effective in engaging the community?

If the activity is successful, what should be the next step? (Each activity should be one step in a journey rather than random happenings.)

When is the best time to conduct the activity? Why?

What is the anticipated outcome of the event or activity?

If the outcome is achieved what impact will it have on the other ministries of the church?

What training is needed for the event or activity to have the best chance of success?

When should the training be conducted?

What is the total budget for the event or activity?

What is the follow-up planned for the event or activity? When?

By whom? Data shared with whom?

Who is responsible for this event or activity? To whom are they responsible?

LEADERSHIP DEVELOPMENT MINISTRY PLAN

Briefly review the Business Plan:

Clarify issues

Answer questions

Determine level of church commitment to and buy-in for the Business Plan

Address the key issues identified in the Business Plan

Leadership Development Ministry Plan: This issue addresses the plan and process the church will utilize to identify, enlist, engage, and equip church members to lead small groups and other ministries.

Goal number of new leaders to deploy according to the Business Plan _____

Evaluation of the current leadership development ministry plan:

What is the method of identifying potential leaders?

What is the method of enlisting potential leaders to fulfill their passion and giftedness?

Are there current job descriptions for the potential leaders?

Is there a leader covenant?

What training is provided to equip potential leaders?

How is the quality of the leader's presentation and follow-up gauged?

Is there a systematic plan of accountability?

Discuss elements of potential leadership development plan

Leader evaluation

How often will evaluations be conducted?

Including what elements?

Dependability

Preparation

Execution

Follow up

Development of mentee

Leader training

How often?

Including what elements?

Doctrine

Presentation

STEWARDSHIP DEVELOPMENT MINISTRY PLAN

Briefly review the Business Plan:

Clarify issues

Answer questions

Determine level of church commitment to and buy-in for the Business Plan

Address the key issues identified in the Business Plan

Stewardship Development Ministry Plan: This issue addresses the plan and process the church will utilize to assist church members and others to understand the elements of stewardship and how stewardship is a vital part of every aspect of church ministry. Specific areas the plan will address are family budgeting, debt reduction, investing and financial planning, and estate planning.

Goal of stewardship process according to the Business Plan ————.

Evaluation of the current stewardship development ministry plan:

Is there currently an ongoing and systematic stewardship plan identifying the areas listed above?

How effective is the stewardship plan in the church?

Discuss elements of potential stewardship development plan.

Budgeting

Training or seminars

Date(s)

Person responsible for scheduling

Preparation

Follow-up

Debt Reduction

Training or seminars

Date(s)

Person responsible for scheduling

Preparation

Follow-up

Investing and Financial Planning

Training or seminars

Date(s)

Person responsible for scheduling

Preparation

Follow-up

Estate Planning

Training or seminars

Date(s)

Person responsible for scheduling

Preparation

Follow-up

PARTNERSHIP DEVELOPMENT MINISTRY PLAN

Briefly review the Business Plan:

Clarify issues

Answer questions

Determine level of church commitment to and buy-in for the Business Plan

Address the key issues identified in the Business Plan

Partnership Development Ministry Plan: This issue addresses the plan and process the church will utilize to identify and engage other churches and entities in a reciprocal expression of the gifts God bestows in the Christian family resulting in strong relationships and an enlarging of the kingdom of God.

Goal of identifying and engaging partners according to the Business Plan _____

Evaluation of the current partnership development ministry plan:

Is the church currently engaged with any other entity in a mutual partnership agreement?

If so, are there covenants in place?

Are there mutually agreed upon outcomes for each partner?

Have the levels of partnership been identified and defined?

Discuss elements of partnership development plan

Partnership is an attitude, a mind-set through which mutual ministry goals can be achieved

Partnership is reciprocal

Partnership is a biblical expression of unity and an appropriate use of God's gifts

Partnership focuses on excellence

Partnership encourages mobilization

In partnership all entities are equal

Partnership belongs to and requires involvement from everyone

Partnership requires excellent communication

Churches must be trained in how to be a partner and how to receive partners in their church

To be an effective partner the church needs a well-defined mission strategy that encompasses their local field but also reaches out to their Judea, Samaria, and the Uttermost. An Acts 1:8 plan is essential to successful partnerships.

✝ NOTES

Bartlett, Gene, *"It Takes Faith"* (Commisioned by Baptist Church Music Conference, 1977).

Collins, Jim, *Good to Great* (New York, NY: HarperCollins Publishers, Inc., 2001).

Mason, Babbie, and Eddie Carswell, *"Trust His Heart"* (Word Music, 1989).

McGavran, Donald, *The Bridges of God: A Study in the Strategy of Missions* (Wipf & Stock Publishers, 2005).

Murphy, James D., *Flawless Execution* (HarperCollins Publishers Inc., 2005).